ALOHA

THE SPIRIT WITHIN YOU

Once you touch a person's heart
with kindness, you leave a lasting
impression no one else can erase.

Dr. Linda Andrade Wheeler

My gratitude is extended to those who
continually share their stories with me,
some of which are included in this book.
They have brought "realness"
and warmth to this book.

Graphic Design and
Photography by:

Joe Hunt
Joe Hunt Design

Published by Po'okela Publishing
1200 Ala Moana Blvd., Space 10, Honolulu, HI 96814
www.successhawaii.com

This book is dedicated to my
eldest son, Milton Wheeler,
who exemplifies the *aloha* spirit
– it's a way of life for him.

PILIALOHA

(friendship)

ʻO ka hoa pili, he kōkoʻolua i ka noho mehameha.

A friend is someone who makes you feel better than being alone.

Contents

HILINA`I

(faith)

`O ka hilina`i ka `imi `ana i kahi pōhihihi a
ka puka aku `ana me ka `ike.

To believe is to reach into the unknown, and to be able
to grab onto something in the process.

FORWARD
by Kumu John Keola Lake

*"Breathe life into others and
bring out the best in them..."*

"*A 'ole i piliwi 'ia* ... Unbelievable!!! At last, one of the
few and rarest but poignant explanations to a beautiful Hawaiian word, *ALOHA*. This simple world-renowned
word of deep meaning and spirituality has finally been
brought to the conscious minds of modern-day
Hawai'i and the world. This little book has undoubted-
ly reached into the depths of Hawaiian thinking and
feeling and finally has been placed into the printed
word to convey the essence of the *aloha* spirit.

To the Hawaiian, man, in essence, is a consummation of knowledge from the past, which gives stability to his path in the present, and secures the hope for a full and valuable future. 'Olelo, word or speech was far more than a means of communicating. To the kupuna, the spoken word did more than set into motion forces of destruction and death, forgiveness and healing. The word itself was "force." The most powerful gift man possesses is his power to communicate. Language puts us in touch with nature; verily, he creates his language from nature. That "alo" or presence is one's physical presence imbued with the life force given by God, the creator, the waters of life, "ka wai ola a Kane". The "ha" or breath of life, as Dr. Wheeler states, is not only the sustaining life force within us as we inhale, but in exhaling, we give life to words, ideas and design.

"Hu wale ka ha, ke ea, ka leo, kani ka ha, kani ke ea, kani ka leo"......
Swell forth the breath, the self-identity, the voice, sound forth the breath, the self-identity and the voice...a line taken from a chant of inspiration.

Being raised in Lahaina by my maternal grandmother who was a manaleo, or native speaker and surrounded by the Hawaiian voices of my paternal grandparents while attending St. Anthony Boys High School, aloha was a revered word for them. All of them were being very strong Christians, so aloha was reserved for their relationship with God, *"aloha ke Akua"*. But the act of *aloha* was a constant factor in their daily living, from sunrise to sunset. Their actions always gave credence to the creator and in their relationship with others. These values and mores were passed on from parent to child and then to their grandchildren, from generation to generation.

As a child growing up with my grandparents, this would be typical everyday conversation displayed in a manner when family, friend or *malihini* would stop by:

Visitor: *Ui! 'O wai ko loko o ka hale, eia ku' u hoa*
           Hey! Who's home? Your friend is here.

Kupuna: *'Ano'ai kaua, aloha mai nei*
           Greeting (to you and me), Love is given

           Pehea kou ola kino?
           How is your health?

Visitor: *He mea ma'a mau,*
           Same as usual
           'eha ka wawae paha
           A little sore feet perhaps,

Kupuna: *Auwe! E kala mai, komo*
           Goodness!, Excuse me, come inside

           Maloko, e noho malie
           Come sit down.

Visitor: *Mahalo no kou lokomaika'i*
               Thank you for your kindness

Kupuna: *Luhi 'oe paha, a polloi no ho'i.*
              You must be tired, and hungry also.

    This short exchange of social graces is epitomized in a wonderful Hawaiian proverb, *"He'e 'epa ke aloha, he kula 'ilua"* ... Love is peculiar;, it pushes in opposite directions – simply stated, love goes two ways, to love and to be loved.[1] And as it always customary to care for the well-being of your guest as seen this *'olelo na'eau:*, *"Ua ola loko i ke aloha"* – Love gives life within; love is imperative to one's mental and physical welfare.

    The late Pilahi Paki, revered *kupuna* from Lahaina, said that the word *aloha* could be used as an acronym for some very sustainable Hawaiian values,

A *Akahai,* being unpretentious, and modest in our actions and deeds;

L *Llokahi,* having balance and harmony in your life with yourself, others and nature;

O *'Olu'olu,* being pleasant and giving comfort;

H *Ha'aha'a,* the state of humbleness, recognizing the life force given by god;, and,

A *Ahonui,* having patience with yourself and with others.

10

The term "Aloha Spirit" is certainly not new to modern day media or the marketing world. It is a prolific phrase that has been satirized, politicized, marketed, editorialized, abused, overused and misused, and almost always failing to understand the precious gift that it implies. To the reader, enjoy this thought-provoking recipe for living one's life with dignity and joy. If you have a gift of *aloha,* share it. As Dr. Wheeler suggests, "the Aloha Spirit is powerful. It can change the way you see yourself, your relationships and your world."

"O ke aloha ke kuleana o kahi malihini" Love is the host in strange lands. In old Hawai'i every passerby was greeted and offered food, whether he was an acquaintance or a total stranger. But the gift one offers is in the gesture and recognition of another person's life force. *Aloha.*

1. Puku'i, Mary Kawena. 'Olelo No'eau, Honolulu: Bishop Museum Press, (1) 556, (2) 2836, (3) 2463.

Aloha: The Spirit Within You

By Dr. Linda Andrade Wheeler

any books have been written about the *aloha* spirit, but the one thing that distinguishes this book from the others is the clarity with which the reader will discover the path to linking with others on a level that will transcend the physical self and awaken the spiritual bonding between human beings.

Here in Hawaii, acts of kindness, friendliness, helpfulness, and genuine caring are referred to as the "aloha spirit." It is a strong emotion that connects people to each other and results in positive, personal relationships. The *aloha* spirit lives within all of us, and we all have the capacity to share that spirit with others. Anyone who has felt the *aloha* spirit is, in turn, motivated to practice and perpetuate it, simply because it nourishes the soul and provides us with feelings of love, joy, and peace. When we share the *aloha* spirit we also boost our self-esteem, promoting goodwill among people, instilling a joyous sense of camaraderie, and inspiring personal excellence.

It is generally agreed upon by those who live in Hawaii that whatever we "throw out" into the universe, primarily in our interactions with people, will eventually come back to us. If this were true, wouldn't we rather promote positive relationships and receive love, joy, and peace in return? The quality of our life should be measured by all the love we give out and all that comes back to us. Sharing the *aloha* spirit is truly one guaranteed way to accomplish that.

Aloha: The Spirit Within You will provide you with the basic principles of living and three simple steps to spread the *aloha* spirit to help you build meaningful relationships. It invites you to examine the quality of your interactions with others and to use your ordinary powers to create extraordinary spiritual links with them.

PAHUHOPU

(goals)

E hoakāka i kou manaʻo, a e nānā pono i nā pahuhopu,
inā nō e hoʻokō ʻia ana.

Be clear in what you want, then give focused attention everyday to getting it.

Chapter 1

Aloha: The Spirit Within You

he essence of the *aloha* spirit is embodied in the word *"aloha"*, which means *"alo"* (in the presence of God) and *"ha"* (the breath of life) – the presence of God is the breath of life. Since we are all born in the likeness of God, we possess an inherent and extraordinary gift of goodness in our souls. We, alone, have the power to nurture and extend this goodness to anyone at anytime, wherever we may be. It is a conscious decision that we make for ourselves. No one else has that power.

As a result, we can all choose to help people live together in understanding, appreciation, and harmony, even though our world is beset with inequalities, injustice, and violence. In our imperfect world, we are faced with many challenges, everywhere and everyday. We see people destroying others – not only in their own homes, and in their communities, but also as we watch as nations wage war with others, half-way around the world. Instead of hurting others, we must concentrate on redirecting our energies and efforts toward helping others. Love and nurture everyone, and the world will be a better place. Each of us can make a real difference by practicing behaviors that foster and promote goodwill toward others. This is the beginning of a truly honorable mission – the promotion of true internal happiness for you and for others, thereby creating a better world.

The word *"aloha"* in our contemporary world means "hello", "good-bye", and "love". Sometimes it is used lightly, but *"aloha"* embodies a much deeper concept. *"Aloha"* is that special feeling of goodness within us that motivates and inspires us to give the best of ourself to others. It is the acknowledgment of all that life has given to us and our willingness to give back to life.

The *aloha* spirit is an extremely powerful concept that can dramatically change our life. When we truly live the *aloha* spirit, we become empowered in recognizing the value of our life and our ability to spread goodness wherever we go. It is this "magic of your soul" which enables us to give to ourself that comes directly from our higher being and our best self. We become incredibly powerful, thereby enabling us to pass the *aloha* spirit on to others, even to those who may not realize that they have it within themselves. You will feel extremely gratified when you can then enable others to discover that gift within themselves, which can result in happiness and serenity in their lives.

The *aloha* spirit is especially powerful because it is contagious, and what we give will come back to us over and over again – sometimes in totally unexpected ways, like a gentle drizzle that blesses us, and at times, like an instant downpour that overwhelms us with its gifts. When we have emotionally and spiritually touched someone, it can take our breath away. Words and actions merge to strengthen the human connection, and it is this powerful force that binds us as human beings.

This is the basic lesson of this book. You cannot connect with another person on a meaningful level if you do not develop the personal power to touch that person's heart and soul. It is this engagement of the heart and the merging of both souls, which create an understanding of each other. That intangible, invisible, but real linkage of goodness, resulting in the *aloha* spirit can then be passed on from one person to another. It is the positive energy that reaches out to nourish all those in its path.

The *aloha* spirit is warmth, trust, respect, and friendship extended to another person for no other reason than to make that person feel special and loved. This gift of *aloha* is something anyone can give to another, but it must be developed and nurtured within you before it can be shared with others. This is something anyone can do. We all know people who have the tremendous gift of finding joy everywhere and then leaving it behind them, wherever they go. We can similarly develop and nurture this spirit of *aloha*, which celebrates life and ultimately can promote goodwill in our world.

And like the person who finds joy everywhere, we must always live the *aloha* spirit with all living being to truly make a lasting and indelible imprint on others. The "golden rule" applies everywhere, no matter where we go: Treat people as we would like to be treated, *only do it first.*"

It is interesting to note that in Hawaii, the `Aloha Spirit', is State Law. The Hawaii Revised Statues, section 5-7.5 was enacted in 1986 to remind citizens, government officials of Hawaii and visitors to the islands to consider the *aloha* spirit as they interact with others.

If we are serious about spreading the *aloha* spirit, we cannot take it lightly. It asks a lot of us. We must nurture and develop the *aloha* spirit and be the best person we can be – giving our best every time to everyone. We alone determine our success. The *aloha* spirit is not a frivolous concept that we just think or talk about. It must be a conscious and consistent action on our part in order for us to fully realize its rewards. It is a powerful concept that we can practice each day of our life. We must have this definite goal –

to give positive thoughts and actions to everyone who comes into our world. We must fuel our passion with a vision of giving the *aloha* spirit, and everything we do must be geared toward the realization of that vision.

I remember so vividly an experience encountered in Venice, Italy. As my husband and I exited the train station and climbed down the steps to board a boat to our hotel, we saw an elderly gentleman playing the violin, as if he were in another world. The beautiful music filled the air in that romantic place where even nonbelievers quickly warm to its charm. The violinist's passion for his music touched me, and I could feel his delight in sharing his gift with us. The music came from his soul. At his feet was the open violin case, which was used to collect any donations from passing tourists. I saw that the tattered and faded black case held only a few coins, so I quickly searched for a crispy twenty-dollar bill and deposited it in the violin case. As the violinist continued playing, I smiled and quietly thanked him for the beautiful music. As soon as my husband and I boarded our boat, the old man stopped playing his violin and looked at the twenty-dollar bill in his case. He picked it up and examined it closely. Then threw me a kiss – Italian style. His joy made me so happy, and it was a special welcome to Venice that I will never forget.

During our visit in Venice, my husband and I met wonderful people who dined with us and shared their own impressions of that wondrous place and tales of their own homelands. It was a wonderful experience, and we loved learning about new and interesting places. In turn, my husband and I shared information about our family and life in Hawaii. We were always pleasantly surprised to discover the similarities in our lives as well as the differences, which made each of us so special.

While traveling on trains in Europe, my husband and I were fascinated as we watched people's expressions and reactions as they conversed in many different languages. Upon leaving Venice, we boarded a train to Nice, France. Two young American women sat close by us and started talking about their experiences in Venice and what they intended to do on their next stop in Milan, on their way to Geneva, Switzerland. As they conversed among themselves, my husband Milt, upon hearing their dilemma as to what to see, do, or taste, introduced himself and shared information on what he had read about Milan. He provided them with information on places, food and other things they wouldn't want to miss, and they were so grateful to have that information. Soon, we had a four-way conversation going and began to talk about ourselves. We were delighted to find that we were all Americans enjoying September in Europe. Both of the women, Stacey and Sarah, lived in San Francisco. Stacey was a medical intern in pediatrics and Sarah had just graduated as a civil engineer. They were fun and interesting, and time went by too quickly. Before long, we arrived at their connecting point – Milan, Italy. Not wanting to see this refreshing experience come to an abrupt end, I searched my carry-on luggage for copies of my book on personal excellence, "*Ain't Life an Artichoke? – It Takes a Lot of Peeling to Get to the Heart of It*", and gave a copy to both women. Then we said our good-byes, and our train proceeded on to France.

Five years later, my husband and I went on a cruise from Vancouver, Canada to various points in Alaska. On the first day of our cruise, we received a handful of gift certificates from our children to celebrate our fortieth wedding anniversary as well our dinner table assignments for the entire trip. Eight people were assigned to our table. We were excited to meet the people we would be seeing each night at dinner. We hoped that the other six people assigned to our table would enliven and enhance our daily dining experience.

That first night, we excitedly dressed for the formal occasion and arrived at the restaurant with great anticipation of meeting six new people. We were one of the first couples to arrive and watched as each pair of vacationers in their evening attire sat at their designated seats, enjoying the freshness of the experience. As the eight of us came face to face with each other, someone suggested that we introduce ourselves.

A'O

(education)

Ke noke 'oe i ke a'o, he 'ikena moakāka ma laila.

Learning is a commitment to new clarity.

When it was our turn, my husband shared information about our family, our business in Hawaii, and what we enjoyed doing. Milt asked me to tell them about my writing, which I gladly did. Then someone asked how I got started writing books, and I gladly shared that story. Stacey, a young woman at the far end of the table, immediately said, "I've heard that story before – from a woman on a train in Europe. I still have her book, *"Ain't Life an Artichoke?"*
"Oh, my God!" I replied. "That's me!"

Stacey said excitedly, "This is incredible. I can't believe it!"

She reported that she and Sarah read my book on the way to Switzerland and they both loved it. Meeting like this was unbelievable. My husband and I were stunned. Nothing like this had ever happened to us before. It was an exhilarating experience for both of us and helped to reaffirm our continuing belief that whatever good we throw out into the universe comes back in wonderful and sometimes mysterious ways.

Stacey's mother, who was a nurse from Dallas, Texas, was her companion on the cruise and mentioned that Stacey had shared that European Train experience with her. Stacey is now a resident in one of the largest hospitals in San Francisco and is known for her work with young children. Her friend Sarah, who had accompanied Stacey on the European jaunt, returned to Europe to work, and was still there. The others at the table were astonished with our story and chance reacquaintance. Happily, that encouraged everyone to share more stories of other interesting incidents that happened to them, and we looked forward to hearing other exciting stories each night.

My husband and I enjoyed a wonderful seven-day cruise in the company of Stacey's beautiful mother – who just happened to be a fellow George Straight fan, so we shared a strong common bond. And although we stayed in different hotels in Vancouver, we continued to bump into Stacey and her mother for the next three days – the candy shop, at a Greek Restaurant, and at a Chinese goods store. We later determined that our friendship was just meant to be. Our meeting on the cruise convinced us that this universe may be huge, but our personal connections truly make it a small, small world.

Chapter II

Basic Principles of Living

 o definition can adequately convey the essence of the *aloha* spirit – it simply transcends any definition. But we can see it and feel it in our interactions with others. To practice it on a daily basis is to know it. It is a gift of self that we can and should give to others. Following some basic principles of living will enable us to share the *aloha* spirit with others.

1.
Breathe life into others and
bring out the best in them.

The *aloha* spirit is a culture that lives within us. It is a unique culture that cannot be seen with our eyes but can be felt with our heart. This culture exists within everyone. However, not all human beings realize their powerful potential to be kind and to touch another person's life in a way that will leave a lasting imprint that no one else can erase. Whenever we come into contact with another human being, we have an incredible opportunity to change that person's life by the kind of individual we choose to be and how we interact with that person.

People sometimes do not recognize or appreciate their own gifts, but we can help them discover their own goodness by telling them what they might not be aware of about themselves – their beautiful smile, their kindness to others, their willingness to help those in need, their uplifting and inspiring stories, etc. We should do our best to touch people's hearts emotionally to awaken the *aloha* spirit within them – that spirit of love and caring that dwells within each of us.

Have you ever noticed how some people bring out the best in us, while others transform us into a person we hardly recognize and ultimately dislike because we are not emotionally comfortable there? Our memories retain these incredible snapshots of all the experiences we've accumulated over the years. Even when I haven't seen a particular face for many years, I somehow instinctively know how that person made me feel when we last met. These experiences are safeguards to our souls, since we naturally gravitate to people who wrap us with their warmth and avoid, as much as possible, the prickly people who make life so difficult and miserable.

At times, we catch ourselves saying positive things about how people make us feel. Have you ever said something like this to yourself: "I like that lady. She makes me feel good. I am not scared to be my true self with her. Somehow she brings out the best in me. I don't know why, but when I'm with her, I am the person I am most proud of." Why did you react in this way? It was probably because this person was able to create a culture where the *aloha* spirit could be exchanged, and the energy of that powerful source surrounded you. It is a wonderful feeling, but more than that, it is even more powerful because it is contagious. We can actually catch that spirit, internalize it, and then share it with another person as frequently as we desire. The Japanese expression *"Okage Sama De"* – I am who I am because of you – testifies to the tremendous impact we can have on another person's life.

Ultimately, what counts most in life is how we feel about ourselves and what we do for others. When we are kind to ourselves, we have a better chance of feeling happy, being comfortable with who we are, and recognizing that getting to our best self is a life-long process, not a temporary one. When we are able to realize this, we will then be able to give others the same understanding and acceptance, and they, in turn, will have a better chance of being who they truly are in our presence. Someone once said that when we first meet a person, it is not really that person we are meeting, but a representative of someone they would like to be. This is probably because they do not know us and therefore do not feel comfortable being their true self. However, when people feel safe in our presence, they can reveal their true self because we are no longer a threat to them.

My mom always told me to make friends, even if I didn't need them. She said that being a friend to others is a gift we give to ourself and that if we are kind to all people, no matter who they are, we will be blessed with the knowledge that we shared our best self with them and invited them to do the same. What a wonderful thought it is to invite others to savor life with people who respect each other and to give everyone the opportunity to be at their best. And if people do not accept our invitation, as it might happen at times, since people are unpredictable, we are still the bigger person for having extended the invitation. We should never forget that. We should invite everyone to our party of life. It is their decision if they choose not to attend.

My longtime colleague and friend, Haroldeen Wakida, was a wonderful person and a great educator. I met her when we both worked for the Hawaii State Department of Education, and we became good friends. At one point in her career, Haroldeen served as President of the Hawaii State Teachers Association (HSTA), and I especially admired her in that role as she oftentimes faced the public and expertly fielded the many questions and concerns from audiences. She was a good listener and became well-informed about on education-related issues. She was an articulate and responsible professional, a good decision-maker, and an impeccable dresser. I truly valued her friendship because in our many discussions, we shared what was closest to our hearts and knew that it would remain between us.

While serving as principal of Aliiolani Elementary School in Kaimuki, Haroldeen fell ill with cancer and struggled through many years of pain with dignity and no self-pity. She held on to hope and life with unwavering strength, and it was always a pleasure to spend time with her. Shortly after her illness had been diagnosed, Haroldeen joined me for lunch at a new Japanese restaurant. When we arrived at 11:30 a.m., we discovered that the restaurant did not open until noon. Fortunately, however, we noticed some nearby shops and quickly decided to grab the opportunity to shop for at least half an hour. So off we went to a dress shop. Haroldeen was an excellent shopper and found a nice outfit that looked terrific on her. She was pleased and wore it to our company's leadership conference the following week.

After making our purchases, we returned to the restaurant and sat at the sushi bar. As we tasted all of the different delicacies, we had fun talking and eating, laughing and sharing. All the while, the sushi chef continued to create and serve us the special rice delicacies, which he had so carefully designed with his talented hands. After nearly two hours of discussion and food, we decided to call it a day and asked for the check. The owner of the restaurant handed me the check with an incredulous look on her face. When

I looked at the bill, I understood why – Haroldeen and I had eaten $150 worth of sushi between the two of us, and we had enjoyed each and every piece! After getting over the shock, I turned to Haroldeen and said, "Ah, Haroldeen, I don't have enough money. Do you have money?" And we laughed until our mascara was soaked with tears. That meal was an experience that both of us never forgot.

About a year after that dining experience, Haroldeen died. The Diamond Head Memorial Park Chapel overflowed with mourners. People waited in line to express their condolences to her family. I waited in that line for nearly an hour, and when I finally reached her daughter Tracey, who is also a friend of mine, we both grieved over our loss. I then met other members of the family. Having never met Haroldeen's husband, I expressed my condolences and introduced myself, noting that Haroldeen and I were good friends. He acknowledged that he knew me. He said, "I've heard all about you and your sushi experience with my wife." I smiled and replied, "Yes, we had so much fun. I'm going to miss her." That night, I knew that I had lost a dear friend, but I was comforted knowing that she had left me with many wonderful memories — she simply lived life to the fullest.

It is in life's lessons that we are finally able to under-stand who we are. We choose our paths amid the challenges and choices, and then change when necessary. It is through these challenges, choices, and changes that we become stronger and better human beings. And while it is nice when people like us, we must always remember that we cannot expect everyone to like us. Still, that should not stop us from giving our best. We alone determine our own attitude and behavior. We should never give that power to someone else, and we should never try to force people to be like us. Realize that we all have gifts and pitfalls that work for or against us, and that we must help others to look for the best in themselves and to take positive actions on their own behalf.

I recently heard a story that best illustrates this concept. An elderly man sat in his backyard watching monarch butterflies take flight as they gently burst through cocoons attached to leaves of the purple crown flower plant. As he celebrated their new life, he noticed one butterfly still struggling to emerge from its cocoon. He watched the struggle for a few minutes and then ran indoors to get a pair of small scissors. He then cut open the cocoon, thereby enabling the butterfly to escape. He was proud that he was able to help this poor butterfly. However, as soon as the butterfly emerged from the cocoon, it fell to the ground and limped along, unable to fly, and eventually the butterfly died. The man was so disturbed by the death of the butterfly that he shared this experience with a neighbor who also loved butterflies. Upon hearing the sad story, his neighbor told him that the butterfly died because it didn't have enough fluid in his wings to fly. The struggle to free itself from the cocoon is a necessary part of its survival because that struggle is nature's way of forcing fluid from the body of the butterfly into its wings, so it would be ready for flight, once it achieves its freedom from the cocoon. This was a valuable lesson. We can help and encourage others, but we cannot do everything for them. We must allow them to learn for themselves, thereby empowering themselves.

2
Use the power within you to connect with another person.

Wherever there is a human being, there is an opportunity for kindness. We should take every opportunity to get to know people, and it will give us the chance to experience the more important things in life – friendship, love, personal satisfaction, etc. The spirit of being and giving is what matters most in life. We should find ways of connecting with people through our career, special interests, hobbies, and other life choices. That human connection is important to enable us to verify who we are and to enable others to validate the vision we hold for ourselves. They help us get to our best self by providing us with feedback. It is a vital link to personal excellence. We cannot be excellent by ourselves.

Life is the only evidence of growth, just as growth is

the only sign of life. To perpetuate life, we must continue to grow in new and better ways. Personal growth
contributes to personal excellence. In order to breathe
life into others, we must develop and use that inner
force – that power of connection. It is only when we
are able to do this, that our spirit can live on, even
when our body dies. This is the magic of our soul. We
should remember the goodness of Princess Pauahi
Bishop, Mother Theresa, Mahatma Gandhi, Martin
Luther King, and all the others whose lives have a special connection to people throughout the world. They
lived the *aloha* spirit, and more importantly, they
inspired others to do the same and to continue to pass
it on to others everyday. We can do this, too. Do not
let the chain of love stop with us.

My father, Lionel Martin Andrade, had a prayer he
created and faithfully recited at the conclusion of our
Catholic mealtime prayer. We loved hearing our father
say the prayer with such meaning and devotion.
Today, 10 years after my father's passing, my nephew,
Chubby Pridgen, keeps the prayer alive at our family
gatherings, when he bows his head to pray, "Dear
Lord, help us to make decisions that are reasonable in
caring, sharing, loving, and forgiving." We all know
that our father's spirit lives within us and that when we
hear that prayer, we are reminded to act on those
words.

I once saw a billboard in Los Angeles that said,

HOʻOKŌ
(accomplishment)
E hilinaʻi ʻoe I kāu hana, a hana pono nō.
Believe in what you do and do it well.

"Caring is Good; But Doing Something is Better". We must do something to get something in return. Nothing begets nothing. When we make people feel good about themselves, they feel good about us. We need to show that we care. People are not interested in how much knowledge we have, who our friends are, or what lifestyle we possess. They care about how we treat them. We must work hard to be a good person and use the power within us to connect with others. Give others the chance to share their best by listening to them as if they were the only people on this earth. It will make them feel special.

I recently attended the wake services of a family friend who maintained such an incredibly positive attitude, even while facing many of life's tragedies. As I listened to the people who spoke about him, I know that Joe would have enjoyed knowing that he had made such a difference in so many lives. He had planted many seeds during his lifetime, and this made his life purposeful and meaningful. And although he witnessed the growth and maturity of many, there were others who "never got it," perhaps because they didn't care enough or perhaps because they thought they were too smart to learn something new. Unfortunately, some people never value what they have until it is gone, and these people sometimes regret their loss the most. Once we have lost something of value, we can either realize and appreciate what we had or we can merely continue to sigh at our losses and lose ourself in the process. We are the only persons who can place a value on anyone or anything. Sometimes it takes only a glance to see the worth of our life. However, sometimes we need to search deep down inside our soul to find that which we value.

Be continually grateful for your life and all its blessings – eating your favorite foods, enjoying good friends, flying a kite, listening to your favorite music, planting a new tree, reading an exciting book, putting on freshly laundered clothes, cradling a sleeping baby, etc. The best things in life do not have a price tag but are given and received free of charge – a welcoming smile, courtesy, kindness, genuine interest, loving thoughts, being there for a friend or even saying a prayer for someone in need. Although absolutely free, these wonderful human exchanges are worth more and have a strong lasting power, which is absolutely priceless.

3.
Be of Service to Others
Whenever you Can

We all need the help of others to survive, be secure, and successful in our lives. Therefore, we should reach out and help others whenever we can. Be quick to give service to those who are in need. Help them to find comfort, strength, and meaning in their lives to enable them to endure the struggles, which they may encounter. People sometimes hesitate to ask for help when they need it, so it is up to us to step forward and support them in their hour of need. Be of good heart, and the support we give may help to change another person's perspective on life. Perhaps they have not experienced kindness from anyone for a long while. Be that person who shows kindness, and through that process of helping, the life we change may very well be our own.

In our small neighborhood in Kahului on the island of Maui, I remember Mr. Ramos, who was eighty-seven years old and who stood in front of his house each morning to wave good-bye to all of his neighbors as they left for school and their jobs. There he was every morning with a big smile on his face and a hearty wave as each neighbor drove past his daughter's house where he lived. He made each of us feel special, as though he was standing there just to see us off. And, late in the afternoon, when all of us returned exhausted from our day's activities, there was Mr. Ramos once again with his refreshing smile and big wave, welcoming us back to our homes. How comforting it was knowing that Mr. Ramos cared enough about each of us to give us our first and last greeting of each day. And although his presence was expected on a daily basis, it was never taken for granted. Many of us told him how much we appreciated his greetings, and this encouraged him to continue his wonderful practice. When he died, a part of us died, too. Something was missing from our lives. Our eyes would automatically take us to the place where he used to stand and wave to us. Because he cared, he gave us hope. He gave back to the community all that he learned about life and taught all of us the power of a smile and a wave. Although he died nearly thirty years ago, Mr. Ramos left a lasting impression on our hearts. His spirit still lives on in that place where he stood with an infectious smile and the big sweep of his arm that showed us that he cared.

We all have gifts to share with others. We should teach people to value each other as human beings and show decency in the things we do for others. Ultimately, each of us will be judged on the basis of the kindness we show others. No one really cares if we turn in all our reports on time, earned the most sales, or built a massive financial portfolio. People will remember our kindness and how we treated them as human beings.

A friend once commented on the dash that is inscribed on tombstones between the birth date and the date of death. She asked, "What is the worth of your dash?" I thought she was joking, but then she explained that although we tend to ignore it, we should really be concentrating on the dash because it represents the entire life of the individual. Her question then took on more meaning, and I began to ponder this idea more seriously. What is most important is the quality of our lives and what we contribute to this world? Were lives changed because we lived? Is the world a better place because we were in it? What can we do to make a difference? The answers to these questions will give us some measure of our worth.

While visiting the home of one of my friends on O'ahu, I noticed an antique koa ukulele in a glass case on a pedestal. It was placed in a prominent place in the living room. The engraved plate read: "To my gifted son, Kawika. To whom much is given, much is expected. You will bring the music to your soul. Love, Dad" It sounded like there was a story behind this, so I asked about it. Kawika explained that his dad had given him the ukulele as a high school graduation gift about fifteen years ago, just months before his dad had suffered a heart attack and died. He explained that his father loved going to auctions everywhere on the island and took great pride in the quality of the items he found and the bargains he was able to get. On one particular day, he went to an old estate auction in Nuuanu. An elderly couple was settling into a retirement community and needed to clean up before moving. They really didn't need the money, so many beautiful items were being auctioned at reasonable prices. It was the best kind of auction – quality items at reasonable prices. The auction was going well. Then the auctioneer put on the block an old worn koa ukulele with two of its strings undone. The auctioneer took a serious look at the instrument and started the bid at fifteen dollars. The first bid was for sixteen dollars and the second at seventeen. With no more bids, the auctioneer was ready to close the deal when a woman who had been bidding high and getting some prized items bid twenty dollars. The auctioneer again began his countdown.

But before he lowered the gavel, an elderly Hawaiian man walked up to the table and picked up the old ukulele. He wiped the ukulele with his *aloha* shirt and fastened the strings, pulling gently on them as he adjusted and tightened them. He then put the ukulele to his ear and tuned the instrument. Satisfied that it was perfectly tuned, he cradled the ukulele in his arms and began playing a beautiful, haunting melody. Everyone watched in amazement. When he completed the song, he put the ukulele down and disappeared into the crowd as quickly as he has appeared. Upon witnessing this incident, Kawika's father could not contain his emotions, and he bid one thousand dollars for the ukulele. When asked why he paid so much for the ukulele, he replied, "It is not the ukulele that I bought, but the lesson that went with it. I'm a father of five children. I want all my children to know this story well. That in life ... it is not the ukulele that will bring alive the music within it. It is their spirit of learning and doing that will bring learning alive, and bring music to the world." He said that the worth of that lesson is priceless.

Chapter III

Three Simple Action Steps to Spread the Aloha Spirit

Step I. Think Positive About People

he *aloha* Spirit is a philosophy that is appropriate in life – as we interact with our family, friends, and colleagues to make that human connection. It represents an opportunity to help people to live together in understanding, appreciation, and harmony. The *aloha* Spirit seeks to move you from "me" to "we" and break down people-made barriers of prejudice, injustices, discrimination, hatred, and jealousy. When we spread the *Aloha* Spirit to others, we must have an honorable purpose – to make others feel good about themselves in our presence. In that kind of personal exchange, differences are accepted and honored. People realize that differences between human beings cannot be clearly attributed to their ethnicity, culture, or color. Differences exist even in the sameness of these attributes. So what makes a human being different from another?

Those who do not appreciate the human connection and all of its rewards, regress to their own comfort levels, interacting only with those similar to them in their ethnicity, socio-economic level, religion, age, etc. — which does not test their true sense of being human; it merely substantiates their presence as a living creature devoid of 'life'. We grow personally when we interact with different people to enhance and enrich our life. Remember that if two people always think alike, what is the use of one? We want diverse and new ideas, thoughts and experiences so that we can grow intellectually, emotionally, socially, mentally, and spiritually – so we can bring balance and excitement to our life.

There are no perfect people in the world. We must learn to accept people exactly as they are. Accept all people because they are in the world with us – each of them has a special place in this world. Know that everybody has gifts and pitfalls. We must ask ourselves, "am I the problem or the solution in my relationships?" Then we must go about adjusting our behavior so that we can add positive energy into our relationships, rather than to sap it of its potential luster.

We see what we look for and what we look for, we usually find. With people, we must look for the best in others and understand what we cannot see. My daughter-in-law, Kim, sent me this wonderful story that serves as a reminder to be more considerate and compassionate in our interpersonal relationships.

A well-known speaker started off his seminar by holding up a crispy twenty-dollar bill. He asked the roomful of 200 people, "Who in here would like the twenty-dollar bill? Hands started going up throughout the room and the speaker said, "I'm going to give this twenty-dollar bill away. But first, watch this." The speaker crumpled up the twenty-dollar bill tightly and asked if anyone still wanted the money. Again, hands went up. "Well," he continued, "what if I do this?" And the speaker dropped the twenty-dollar bill on the floor, crumpled and dirty. "Anyone still want it?" he asked. Again, all the hands went up, although some were becoming skeptical. "You all have learned a valuable lesson here." He continued, "No matter what I did to this money, you all still wanted it because it did not decrease in value. It is still worth twenty-dollars, no matter if it is ragged and crumpled."

Many times in our life, we feel like we have been dropped, crumpled and ground into the dirt by the decisions we make and the circumstances that come our way. We feel that we are worthless. But no matter what has happened or what will happen, we will never lose our value, dirty or clean, crumpled or carefully creased – we are still priceless to those who love us.

Unlike the twenty-dollar bill, we often increase in

HOPENA

(destiny)

Aia iā ʻoe ka hopena o kou ola, a ma hāʻawi aku i kēlā mana iā haʻi. ʻO kou ola nō kēia, nāu e koho i ka hopena.

Where you intend to end up in this world is entirely up to you. Don't give your power to create your future to someone else. You have only one life to live. Make the best of it.

value by our life's challenges and struggles. The worth of our life is measured by who we are – not what we do or who we know.

Communicate with respect, clarity, and interest. Many of us find it difficult to say what we mean or to express what we feel. We assume that other people understand what we mean. To communicate our meaning effectively, we must have a clear picture in our mind of what we are trying to express and be able to clarify and elaborate on it.

It is said that words are the voice of the heart – that words are filtered through our heart, while our eyes are the windows to the soul. When we speak, we show how our filter is functioning – whether it is clogged with junk (discrimination, prejudice, hate, jealously, feelings of superiority, etc.) or flowing with *aloha* (honesty, trust, compassion, caring, pure thoughts, etc.) Any kind of language that denigrates or demeans people is rude and unkind – and in some instances, illegal. Swearing, calling others names, racial slurs, put-downs and bullying are barriers to positive interactions with others; they are culprits of dysfunctional relationships and have no place in the construction of healthy, meaningful relationships. We all have our own filters and must check them out periodically, to ensure that they function on our behalf — that stereotyping, labeling, assumptions, and other negative thoughts are eliminated, thereby creating space for new thoughts that appreciate and value the contributions and gifts of other people.

If others hold those negative thoughts about us, we must counter those thoughts by being the best person possible. Take responsibility for caring about yourself and others. We should help people whenever we can. This is establishing our own personal insurance policy because when people like us, they will help us to succeed. If they don't like us, they don't care if we fail. It is very hard to dislike someone who likes us and makes life easier for us. We should be that kind of a person to others.

Some might say that language is confusing and limiting because of the different meanings of the words in different contexts. However, language is very powerful in that we often say more than we intend. Even in moments of 'out-of-awareness', when words automatically slip from our tongue, we influence those who receive these words – whether we intended to or not. Make sure you are clear in your intent,... and work on it continuously so you can have the positive effect on people.

There are words that incite hate and violence. In fact, history has shown that words of hate can turn into acts of violence. We must understand the power of words and use language that will support and nurture people, instead of defaming them. Sometimes, it is not what words we know, but what we do with them.

We should give people the opportunity and the support to excel in our presence. Using pedestal words to raise people to a level above the ordinary, exhibits an interest in their ideas.

- May I? Asking permission implies authority.
- I'd like your advice. Suggests superior wisdom.
- You are so kind to spare time from your busy day. Implies he or she is a busy and therefore important person.
- I appreciate getting help from a person of your standing. No one knows just what standing means, but everyone believes or hopes – he or she has it.
- As you probably know. Implies knowledge
- You're right. A pat on the back.
- I'd like your opinion. People on pedestals are supposed to have opinions, so if an opinion is asked of you, you must be up there somewhere.
- Please. A great lubricator for human relations.
- Finally, four little words that aren't heard often enough: You may be right.

Small talk, such as: "Hi! How are you?", or "Hello! What's your name?"or, "Wow! Did you see what just happened, isn't that incredible?", or "I heard you visited Kona last week. What did you do there?" can build big long-lasting bridges to friendship. People do feel good when you are interested in them. They also like it when you make them feel comfortable in your presence. Always know whom you are talking to and respond in ways that make the person comfortable in responding and sharing. Show you care about people by actively listening to them. People do not care how much we know until they know we care about them.

The heart of communication is language, both verbal and non-verbal – so we should be aware of our body language as we express our feelings, thoughts, or ideas. To establish credibility, we should be sure that what we say is what we do. People hear what we say and then they watch to see if we follow through with our actions. Words are cheap – it is through our actions that others will believe the words we use with them. That's how they get to know who we are and what kind of a person we are. Only through our actions will people come to know who we truly are. It is the only measure of our integrity – our worth.

Effective communication is characterized by openness and honesty, trust, understanding, receptivity to other points of view, and congruence between what is said and what is done.

It involves people's attitudes, feelings, relationships,

knowledge, and skills. Therefore, we should never make assumptions about people's understanding of how we communicate. Oftentimes, when we think that we are being clear, we aren't, and others may not understand us. People may want to understand us, but they see or hear things from their own perspectives, not ours. So, one of the things we must understand is that people's perceptions are important in understanding how to effectively communicate with them.

Every one of us lives in a private world of experience; therefore, our perceptions come with all that we've experienced. So, if we want to be understood by people, we need to understand where they are coming from and how they may perceive matters. Be understanding, considerate, compassionate and patient. We may all live in the same world, but we all have diverse patterns of living our lives. Ask questions so that you know if a shared meaning took place. Then and only then, will you know if your message got through.

Step 3.
Act Responsibly.

People are the problems and solutions to every human endeavor. They may also be our biggest frustration or greatest joy. We should examine which relationships in our life are working effectively and which ones are not. And then we should ask ourself, "Am I part of the problem or part of the solution?" If we are not part of the solution, we need to adjust our behavior so that we can improve our relationship or situation – because every relationship that we build or destroy is always our own.

We all come from different cultures, lifestyles and backgrounds. But the culture inside of us is our own creation – it is what we feel with our hearts, think with our heads, and how we act with our bodies. Be accountable for our actions. Remember, people may not believe what we say, but they will always believe what we do. Our actions are the best interpreters of our thoughts. Be responsible.

Who we are and how we act conveys a strong message as to the person that we are. We are what we repeatedly do – and those actions become our habits. We do make a difference by being the very best person that we can be – so we should be the difference and make a difference. Who we are, what we do, and how we go about doing it, has great influence on those who come into contact with us.

As we grow older, we will find that there are nicer people in this world. Even people whom we may have found annoying or downright irritating do not seem to bother us so much anymore. We discover that many of the people we did not particularly like really aren't as bad as we thought. Perhaps because of life's lessons, we have become a bit smarter about our personal power to control our actions, difficult people, and the knowledge that life is designed to make us better, not bitter. We begin to understand that some people have had rougher paths on their journey in life and we make allowances for that. Then there are those who come to appreciate the change in the way we react to them, and it makes them friendlier towards us. Life becomes easier, friendlier and more enjoyable when we realize this. We learn to forgive (forgiving is the first step in healing past hurts) and for-get (nature's great gift of eliminating 'junk' from our life – which only we can do). If we do not learn this, we will miss out on the warmth and friendships we might enjoy.

I'm reminded of a man I met during Christmas time about two years ago as I was autographing some books. He looked older than his sixty-five years, walked with a limp, and looked tattered and sad. As he came closer to me, he told me that all his life people called him "good for nothing" and treated him badly. "Really," I replied. "Why would they do that?" "Well," he replied, "I wasn't nice to them, either." "There you go," I said. "You know you have to give out good stuff to get it back. You must learn to be kind." It seemed to me that this man blamed everyone else for what he couldn't do in his life – to connect with others effec-tively. We need to continually remind ourself that life is not all positive and happy. Life brings us It's lessons, but we can control the way we handle and use these lessons.

Several years ago, I attended a conference in Rapid City, South Dakota. While there, I had the good fortune to attend a huge celebration of dance and culture of the Native American Lakota Indians. The performances were spectacular, and I was awed by the magnificent attire and dances performed by the Native American Indians of all ages. This celebration left a lasting impression on my life. One of the things I never forgot was the huge banner that hung at the entry of the auditorium where this event took place. The sign read, "Good Spirits, Bad Spirits, Your Choice!" It conveyed to me that the *aloha* spirit, as we know it in Hawaii, exists everywhere with everyone. We take our spirits with us and spread them to it with others everywhere we go. It is always your choice, no one else makes that decision but you. And when you decide to spread good spirits, somehow you experience nicer people in life.

Attitudes are habits of thought that predict or perpetuate our performance in life. We choose our attitude, and that is what shapes us. Choices are attitudes, and they become who we are. Everyday we make the choice as to what our attitude will be and how our day will go with everyone. Make choices that will work for us, not against us.

I am reminded of a wonderful story of an architect who was doing a study on cathedrals throughout the United States. As he visited the cathedrals, he noticed one common thing among them – they all had a golden telephone affixed on a wall, with a plaque beneath it, which read, "$10,000 Phone Call to Heaven". The architect saw the same sign throughout the 49 States. When he visited the cathedrals in Hawaii -the 50th State - he noticed that they too had a golden telephone on the wall. However, on the plaque it said, "$.50 Phone call to Heaven". Puzzled, he asked the reverend, "Why is there a difference in price from the mainland for the phone call to Heaven.?" The reverend replied, "Don't you know? It's just a local call from here." As a person who was born and raised in Hawaii, I am convinced that Hawaii is the nearest thing to Heaven, and that we must be grateful every morning as we wake up in this beautiful place we call home. Waking up alive everyday in paradise does count!

Develop and practice habits of the heart – caring, sharing, helping, forgiving, and loving. Help people to feel good about themselves. Help to bring hope into people's lives. If they are able to see opportunities and possibilities, then there can be hope. Sometimes we are victims of our own habits – by perpetuating self-sabotaging behaviors that leave us disconnected from others. We must re-examine our actions so that what we do has a positive impact on people's lives.

Learn the right behaviors that will develop positive relationships and then practice those behaviors. If we do not practice them, we do not learn them. A Japanese proverb says it best, "To know and not to act is not to know at all."

Exhibit the behaviors that you want to see in others. They may not know what the right behaviors are, and you will be helping them to develop new people skills. Also, we should help people to understand that self-sabotaging behaviors are unproductive and can be changed. Have them be accountable for their own actions, rather than letting them complain, criticize, or blame others for their shortcomings – you will be helping them to be better human beings.

The highest compliment we can give another human being is to expect the very best of them, based on our faith and belief in them. To be kind to them is the highest form of that recognition.

To be effective with people, we should start practicing all the genuinely right behaviors with our family – these are the people who will love and care about us, long after other relationships have ended. They will love us, despite our mistakes and our trespasses against them. We can't choose our family (that is God's gift to us), so the best thing is to get to know them and help to take care of them. They will always be our family – no matter how hard we might try to shake some of them off the family tree. They share the roots of our tree. They are forever! If they are not taken care of, they die – and eventually we die an emotional death. It is best to take care of our family. They strengthen our roots, enlighten our spirit of love, foster our personal growth, and can give meaning and purpose to our life.

I have learned that love is a flower that blooms in all seasons. If for some reason, it withers and lies dormant in a season of our life – we shouldn't fret! For love is the everlasting flower that, when retouched, it will bloom again – at times, more profusely than before. We should always have hope in love – it is the only thing that will save us.

One of my colleagues, whose elderly father had passed away, was sharing how wonderful he was as a father and what a wonderful feeling it was for her to have had so much time with her dad. She never once cried while she talked of the special times spent with her father on fishing trips, and then caring for him in his last years. Another colleague listening to the story asked her, "Don't you miss your dad?" Nancy responded immediately, "Of course, I miss him. But his spirit is always with me wherever I go, and it is a good spirit, because I was always kind to my dad and loved caring for him – and he knew it. " She said that it gave her great pleasure, knowing she made his life so enjoyable and worthwhile. What a wonderful gift to give

NA`A U

(attitude)

`O ka mana`o he mea nui o ke ola. `O ia ka mana i
loko ou e kāko`o `ia ai `oe no ka pono.

Attitude determines how well you do the thing you do in life. It is that powerful
message within you that propels you to personal excellence.

anyone – especially a parent!

Once I heard a seminar leader tell the audience that he couldn't understand why, on our birthdays, our parents gave us gifts. He said that he thought that parents should be the recipients of gifts on their children's birthdays. Hearing that, I thought, "That makes sense." Try that. We should consider giving our parents a gift from us on our birthdays and thank them for giving us life (watch their surprise and astonishment at your thoughtfulness). God's gift to your parents was you. How they take care of their gift (you) will be their gift to God. If they have taken good care of you, show them that you appreciate their efforts.

We have the power to act differently when we perceive life and the people in it with the proper perspective. Someone once said, "You see what you look for, and what you look for, you find." Where our attention goes, our energies will follow. We must see people as having special gifts to share, look for that gift within them and most likely, we will find it. We really make the difference in how we see anything or anybody – and what we do about it.

Conclusion:

We can be an ambassador of *aloha*, no matter where we are — we can spread the *aloha* spirit. It lives within us. We have the capacity to transform our life and bring joy to other people's lives. Transform our spirits —

the magic of who we are — into positive actions with everyone, everyday, everywhere. It will be the emotional and spiritual glue that will hold our relationships together.

The *aloha* spirit is powerful! It can change the way we see ourselves, our relationships, and our world. Every time we give the gift of *aloha* to another person, we make it possible to share the human experience – that personal connection with another human being. When we share the *aloha* spirit, we bring a good feeling with us wherever we go, and to those who surround us. We come closer to a world of peace and love in that simple act of sharing your best with someone else.

It starts with us.

Stories of People With Aloha

Marie Achi

"A real estate agent who loves to take care of others because she believes it's just the right thing to do."

While other people may say they care about others, Marie Achi takes it one step further. She actually goes about her days, doing caring things for her family, friends, neighbors and total strangers. Her way of feeling good about herself is to be helpful to others.

She has always been a caring person. It is not a new thing in her life, but her caring is becoming more apparent in new and different ways as she finds her life in full bloom and extend her caring to more people.

Marie Achi grew up in the sugar plantation town of Puunene, the granddaughter of two immigrants. Her dad's father was from Portugal and her mother's father from the Philippines. Her hard-working dad and his father, were long-time supervisors at the Puunene Sugar Mill. They worked with a diverse group of individuals and were both held in high esteem for their treatment of others. Marie's beautiful and gregarious Eurasian mother, a housewife who was raised by an extremely kind Portuguese mother in the plantation village, was the source of inspiration that taught Marie the people skills and developed her capacity to care about others. Her parents and grandparents fueled her desire to help others with challenges in their own lives and to demonstrate her compassion and respect for others.

Throughout her life, her generosity with her time and money was apparent. As the eldest of five girls, she took on the responsibility of tutoring her younger sisters in economics, household chores, education, and love. It wasn't anything she said; it was just what she did. When her parents died, she assumed the role of parent to her sisters and watched each of them mature and raise their own families. She was always there if any sister needed her help – they all knew that.

Marie's life was a tapestry of emotions – happiness, sadness, grief, disappointments, and heartaches. However, through it all, she never faltered in caring about the next person. What impressed me as I watched her leave one marriage and go to another was the way she treated both spouses – with such dignity and caring.

Marie's ex-husband Bill Pridgen, to whom she had been married for twenty plus years on Maui, decided that, after his retirement from Hawaiian Telephone Company, he and his new wife would return to settle in his hometown in South Carolina, where most of his family resided. However, after a few months there, Bill had a stroke and was unable to talk or walk. It was a challenging time for Bill, who was such a fun-loving person. Eventually, his wife Cathy left him in South Carolina and returned to Maui. When Marie heard about this situation, Marie summoned her eldest son, Lionel Eric, who also lived in South Carolina to help his dad. After a year, Bill worsened and even his own brothers and sisters, who lived close to Bill's residence, were unable to help him. Marie and her new spouse Morton Achi and younger son William traveled to South Carolina to assess the situation and convinced her ex-husband to come back to Maui, which he loved, with the promise that they would be his caretakers.

Once on Maui, they arranged for him to get round-the-clock care at a wonderful nursing home on Maui. He loved it. With the return of his eldest son Lionel Eric to Maui, Bill then has his two sons close by to visit him

on a regular basis. Marie and her spouse made frequent visits to Bill, bringing him the foods he enjoyed
and magazines that he loved reading.

My husband and I joined Marie and her spouse on
one of those visits to the nursing home. As we entered
Bill's room, he motioned to Marie that his watch wasn't
working. She went over to him to see what the problem was, but as she grabbed his hand to look at the
watch, Bill pointed to Marie's spouse, Morton, and
asked him take a look at his watch. As I watched,
Morton lifted Bill's hand with kindness to talk to him
about the watch, "Well Bill, looks like we're going to
have to get new batteries for your watch. Let me
have it, and I'll go fix it for you." As I watched this act
of kindness by two men who loved my sister, I won-
dered, "How did she get both of them to be so nice to
each other." Of course, I remembered her capacity
for forgiving and loving and knew that she had passed
that on to them.

At one point in her life, Marie was faced with three
tragedies – all within one year – a burden that would
break any person. In December 2002 during a week-
end party on Maui just three days before Christmas,
her eldest son Lionel Eric, who had just returned from
the mainland after 15 years, died of heart failure – a
condition that had plagued his young life. Marie was
devastated but single-handedly handled all of the
funeral arrangements to be sure it was a fitting send-

off for the son she loved so dearly.

In early December 2003, Bill Pridgen died at the nursing home while her husband Morton Achi struggled for his life in his fight against cancer at the Maui Memorial Hospital. Marie worried for her youngest son William, who was so attached to his dad, and gave him the love and nurturing only a mother could provide.
Seven days after Bill's death, Morton died at the Maui Memorial Hospital. Marie's life had come to a standstill, but her caring and love did not. She embraced all of Morton's family from Honolulu and the mainland, took care of them at their home throughout the services, shared his stuff with his brothers and his children, and gave them the caring attention a grieving family needs.

In the aftermath of arranging for two funerals, Marie took some time to grieve on her own. But this time was short-lived. Mark Rubarth, who shared Morton's hospital room – a forty-nine year old, six-foot seven, mainland transplant from California – needed her help. Dying of cancer, Mark was getting worse and was unable to pay the hospital bills to get the care he needed. Marie – five foot two and a hundred and fifteen pounds — rushed to his aid. Since he was unable to walk, Marie converted her garage downstairs into a hospital room – equipped with a hospital bed and other essential needs to make Mark comfortable during his stay there. She even asked Lori Anderson, one of her friends from Hana, to stay with her so that they both could help Mark move from one place to the next. Marie even arranged for nurses to visit him and take care of his medical needs. Eventually, she arranged for him to be cared for at a nearby nursing home.

As Mark's condition worsened, Marie invited Mark's mother, Donna Lynn Yates, from California to stay with her while she visited her son. Mark's brother, Scott Rubarth, a college professor from Rollins College, Florida, came to take his brother home to California, and he too, stayed at Marie's home, enjoying her hospitality and sumptuous island-style cooking.

During one of Mark's last nights in Hawaii, he inquired where he could get some cigarette lighters with the word Maui printed on it. Marie said that perhaps the service stations or Seven-Eleven stores might have them. So, Lori and Marie laboriously put Mark in the back of her car and drove all around Maui till the wee hours of the morning looking for the specific kind of cigarette lighters that Mark wanted. They stopped only after they found the lighters. When Marie and Lori retell this story, it is clear that they felt so wonderful about what they had done for Mark. He was so happy to be going back to California with those lighters – his present to the people he cared about at home.

During the next months, she kept in close touch by phone with Mark. They talked about the beautiful days he spent on Maui and how much he appreciated her friendship and help. In early August, 2004, Mark died – knowing that he was genuinely cared for and that the Maui angels (Marie and Lori) were looking out for him. Marie said she thought about Mark all that day and what a beautiful person he was. That same day in Hana, Lori called Marie to say that she had strung a beautiful lei for Mark and had taken it to a cliff at the ocean's edge and tossed it into the waves to send her *aloha* to Mark.

Marie's brand of caring reminded me of a campaign banner, I had continuously seen as I traveled around the various sections of Los Angeles. The banner read, "Caring is good. But doing something is better!" The first person I thought of was my sister, Marie Achi. For anyone who knows Marie, she doesn't just talk caring, she does it. What better way of spreading the *Aloha* Spirit then to actually live it all the time? Marie Achi would say, "It's just the right thing to do."

Ron Bright

"*Surrounded by the make-believe world of stage lights, props, and actors who enact writers' words, Ron's devotion and dedication to his craft have made people's dreams come true In real life.*"

Ron Bright is an extremely talented educator who has taught Music, Drama/Theater for over 30 years and has 47 years experience in the theater. His work with youth and theater has brought him national acclaim on the quality of his productions. When he retired from the Hawaii State Department of Education in 1993 at Castle High School, people hoped that it wouldn't affect his involvement in staging plays involving youth. They were elated when Ron came out of retirement to serve as the director of the Castle Performing Arts Center (CPAC) – where their children would have a chance to learn theatre and perform for the community.

For kids from fifth grade to the 12th grade, CPAC is a place where their dreams — of acting, singing or dancing — can be fulfilled. At one time, there was even speculation that families were moving to the Windward side of Oahu so they could take advantage of the CPAC program. This program is a safe haven where talent reigns, but where a student's feelings of disappointment in not having been cast in a particular role are handled with care, compassion, and lots of communication with Ron so that they fully understand the importance of each cast member's contributions to the show, whatever role they portray. Also, Ron invites the parents to be an integral part of the production by watching the auditions and rehearsals and by getting involved in helping with the costumes, scenery, security, or as ushers. Today, Ron is contracted to produce the annual show, featuring 5th through 8th grade students.

During the late 1980's, Ron coordinated stage performances of 1,150 elementary and intermediate students from the Castle Complex Performing Arts Learning Center. It was part of a learning center pilot project in the Castle High School Complex that invited younger students to become involved in the theater.

As the drama instructor for the project, Ron coordinated a glowing performance of sixty students in "Star-Spangled Broadway." He was instrumental in giving his students many opportunities to display their musical and acting talents at educational and community events.

When asked why he puts his heart and soul into his work with students, Ron is quick to answer that he loves kids. First, he loves them; secondly, he teaches them. His ability to connect with them from the heart is his greatest asset. That has always been his goal. Ron says, "As a teacher and drama instructor, I shared the 'spirit' within me to connect with my students. I am convinced that students may not always remember what I taught them, but they will never forget how they felt while in my presence." His strategy was to get close to his students so that they could get to know that he cared about them. Once they knew that, they would produce for Ron because they wanted to make him feel good about them.

You can't be around Ron without laughing and having a good time. He has a genuinely hearty laugh, which is contagious. Combine that with his twinkling eyes and friendly disposition, and you feel safe in his presence – you know that here's a person who will not hurt you but will help you to soar beyond your imagination if you put in the necessary work to do it. He is a firm believer in uplifting spirits with a healthy sense of

KOHO
(choices)

Nāu nō ke koho hopena. E koho pono ʻoe.

You are who you are by the choices you make. Be thoughtful in what you choose.

humor. He says, "Never underestimate the power of a laugh; it's a wonderful connector with people." Perhaps this is the secret to his enjoyment in doing what he does best – helping people to bring out the best in them – while enjoying the moments spent with them.

One day, while in conversation with Ron and his wife, and Mo outside our store at Ward Centre, three people came out of Borders Bookstore located next door to us, and walked straight towards Ron and Mo and warmly hugged them. It was one of his former Castle High School students from years back, who was about to be involved as a dancer in one of the new Broadway shows in New York. They talked about his visit home and how his mom was going to join him in New York to take in the show. The young man shared how he had traveled to Europe for a show and was thrilled to be back on the New York Broadway scene, where he frequently performed. "Wow!" I said, "Terrific isn't it, when your students come back to share what they are up to in their careers." Ron and Mo nodded and said that many of their students keep in touch with them to let them know where they are and what they are doing. They said they had at least 13 former students involved in New York theater shows since Miss Saigon opened, and others who worked in various aspects of production in Las Vegas, Hollywood, Europe and Asia.

Today, out of retirement for the second time, Ron forges forward with the same level of passion for the theater and has broadened his valuable theatrical skills to more experienced actors, as well as students with productions such as *Bye Bye Birdie, Nunsense,* and "*Big River*".

When asked if he played any instrument, Ron replied, "I have rhythm in my soul. He plays the piano by notes, but adds "If I know the melody, I can play any song". He has theater in his heart, and it's been there for a very long time – since the 1950's when he was involved in the Beretania Follies Theatre where he entertained seven days a week, two to three shows a day, while going to school to become a teacher. However, his full schedule didn't deter him from joining the National Guard where he started as a private and ended up as a Master Sergeant. .

For his continuing work with youth and theater, Ron was named a Hawaii Living Treasure by the Honpu Hongwanji Mission. There is even a theater in his name at Castle High School in Kaneohe. Certainly, this extraordinary educator and drama instructor with lots of *aloha* for people who want to be in theater, contin- ues to produce shows that give them the opportunity to realize their dreams.

As Ron claims, putting on stage productions is a Bright affair. His whole family is involved. Mo, his wife of 44 years is his North Star – constantly and continuously shining in his life. She handles the publicity, programs, and props for the shows. His sons Michael and Clark help in whatever capacity they are able – Michael contributes to the show by singing and playing musical instruments in the band, and Clark has conducted the orchestra in many of his father's productions. Today, Ron's *mo'opuna* (grandkids) are anxiously awaiting their appearance in one of their grandfather's productions. It seems that the lights will continue to shine 'Bright' on stage.

Robert Cazimero

*"A gifted musician and singer whose music
eloquently speaks the language of love
and conveys the spirit of aloha."*

He is a world-class entertainer who has traveled the globe, delighting audiences with his melodic voice. A *kumu hula,* he has instilled grace and class in the members of his *halau* to develop them into an elite hula dancing troupe from Oahu. Robert is one half of a famous musical duo, the Brothers Cazimero, who have touched the world with their island songs that speak the language of *aloha.* He is a living legend on a musical journey that began in the late 1960's into the mid-1970's, when he was part of the Sunday

Manoa group, with his brother Roland and Peter Moon. Their group was on the forefront of the Hawaiian Renaissance in music, and today the talented Robert Cazimero continues his cutting edge, musical trek as part of the Brothers Cazimero. However, one of the most remarkable things about Robert Cazimero is his stately presence, which is one of elegance and eloquence, befitting a true gentleman, on stage and off.

Having been in his audience on numerous occasions, and watching Robert's spirit soar through the audience, I was struck with the feeling that he was actually talking and singing to me, when in reality, he was addressing all the others in the audience, of which I was a part. I was curious as to how he is able to make people feel so comfortable, even as he is so passionately engaged in his music or sharing a story. When I asked Robert about this gift of connection with his audience, his reply to me was that it was a learned process. Robert said that it was all about learning how to do it with the grace and style of a professional entertainer. He believes that when you are honest with yourself and comfortable about whom you are, you are most likely to convey that feeling to the audience. He acknowledges that, even if he makes a mistake, he corrects it, which gives the audience the feeling that he is just as human as they are."They like that," he reports.

Robert shared that he was fortunate to have two significant people in his life — his *kumu hula*, Mai'ki aiu Lake and Hawaii's Lady of Song, Loyal Garner — whom he considered to be his valuable mentors who passed on valuable lessons about maximizing the gifts he was blessed with and sharing those gifts with others. He has never forgotten their words of wisdom as they worked with him and other performers, but it was their actions that impressed him the most. Robert said that, by being a good observer, he has learned a great deal from watching them in their personal interactions and professional performances.

It is this spirit of giving to which Robert dedicates himself. It is in this way that he expects and gets the best from others, especially those 'under his wing'. Robert shared that his technique in helping others develop themselves is to humble himself and give them the opportunities to learn so they can improve and get better. He believes that it is easier to break down a person rather than build a person up, but he is a firm believer that, if you build your reservoir of caring and patience to help a person to improve, the person will get stronger and better. Robert admits that, when he learned to step back from his ego and let the pure energy rise to a higher spirit, it was then that he could constructively elevate people and help them in their chosen paths.

It is undeniable that the source of power within

Robert comes from a higher spirit. He acknowledges and is comforted by the greatness of a higher power each time he walks through a lush terrain picking ferns, feels the gentle breeze upon his skin, or observes the goodness in others. Robert pointed out that he lives his life in perpetual gratitude for the opportunities that have come his way, and the successes he has experienced. While he acknowledges that he has been lucky to be in the right place at the right time, he is quick to observe that somebody next to him, his brother Roland, has helped him get there. Robert also knows that his life — in particular — his musical journey, is a miracle inspired by a higher power.

Admittedly, Robert's tenacity, his commitment to his craft, and his focus on continually challenging himself to perfect himself is impressive. Nobody gets to his level of personal excellence without the desire, discipline, and dedication to his craft. However, Robert is quick to point out that, what gave him the long-lasting admiration of his fans was that he was astute in recognizing the tremendous gift that had been bestowed upon him early into his career. As Robert relates, one day as he was recording the song, "*Queen's Jubilee*" as part of *Sunday Manoa's* second album "*Guava Jam,*" he realized the power of his gift of song. As he listened to the replay of the recording, he glanced at a mirror that was on the wall beside him. As he saw the reflection of himself in the mirror, he realized that the voice in the recording was merely an instrument on loan from a higher power to the person he saw in the mirror— himself. That, according to Robert, was the greatest "wake-up moment" in his life; stepping back from his ego and acknowledging that the pure energy and talent that was coming through him was truly a gift from a higher spirit. It is often said that god's gift to us is life, what we make of that life is our gift to god. Robert convinced himself that he was going to make the best of his valuable gift – the gift of song.

Even today, as a renowned singer, giving his best to others is something that Robert consciously does each time he performs. It is something he has practiced and perfected. It is about giving back as far as Robert is concerned. Robert says it is his way of honoring his *kumu hula,* Mai'ki aiu Lake, who unwrapped the gift within him and showed him the way to share it with others. As any fan of Robert Cazimero can tell you, the true recipient of his gift is the audience. What better gift can any audience receive from a world-class entertainer than the gift of *aloha* in song?

Gayle Harimoto

"A generous lei maker, whose true giving does not focus on the return, she focuses on the gift."

The expression, "good things come in small packages" is a truism when it comes to Gayle Harimoto. Not even five feet tall, this personable and talented woman has made a lasting imprint on many people's lives with her gift of *aloha*.

It started many years ago when Gayle began to make and give crown flower leis to performers in local stage shows. It made her happy to see that people really enjoyed her leis. So, she continued to give leis to others, until it became a tradition for her.

One day, Gayle saw a lei made with only the petals of the crown flower. It was beautiful and striking. She inspected it carefully, noting how it was put together, and knew that it would take many hours of work to create such a unique lei. However, she decided to try and make one. The finished lei created quite a stir, and she knew she would continue making her unique leis.

The tedious task of creating the crown flower petal lei is a labor of love. The flowers of the purple crown flower must be picked at just the right stage of blooming. The crowns and petals must then be delicately separated and the petals stored in the refrigerator for a day or two before they can be sewn. The total process involves about 8 hours of work to create one lei. But this did not curb Gayle's enthusiasm for producing such a coveted gift. And when anyone receives this lei, they know that they are very special indeed.

Incredibly, Gayle has no crown flower plants in her own yard. She has established lasting relationships with neighbors who do have the plant in their yards and allow her to pick their flowers on a daily basis. Gayle says she enjoys this stage of the lei-making process because she has gotten to know her neighbors better, not only those with the crown flower plants, but many other neighbors as well as they come out to "talk story," while she is picking the flowers.

The joy of seeing a person's reaction when he or she receives the lei is the reward Gayle gets each time she presents a petal lei to a friend or even a stranger. This is what motivates her to spend the many hours picking, preparing, and sewing the 1,000 petals needed to create each lei. This is also one of the longest-lasting leis — at least 3 weeks if refrigerated.

It doesn't matter what name we give to Gayle's signature lei– the snake lei, the royal crown lei, or the crown petal lei – it is still undeniably a Gayle Harimoto creation and a gift of incredible beauty. And to top it off, Gayle does not accept payment for her leis. Anyone who orders a lei is asked to make a donation to the Aloha United Way, and Gayle forwards the donation to that agency. She says that if she accepted payment for herself, making the lei would then become work and creating the lei would no longer be fun.

Gayle has established many relationships with others through her gift of leis, even with strangers who were fortunate to get one from someone who considered them special. One such person is Alvin Soares, a retired Maui educator, who was honored for his community service about two years ago. On that occasion, he received one of Gayle's leis from me and was so impressed with it that he wrote a letter of thank you to me and Gayle as well. He and his wife, Isabella, met the artistic lei maker when she visited Maui.

Subsequently, when one of his nieces graduated from the University of Hawaii with her degree in education, Alvin was so proud of her accomplishment that he wanted to present her with something special on the morning of her graduation. So, he ordered one of Gayle's lei, which made a real impact on his niece's graduation day. His niece was so taken by the lei that she wrote Gayle to thank her for making such a beautiful lei.

Some of the people who have been touched by Gayle's gift of her lei include: professional skater Kristi Yamaguchi; TV anchor Jodi Leong; writer Lee Cataluna; singers Kuuipo Kumukahi, Hulu Lindsey, Nina Kealiiwahamana, Karen Keawehawaii, Robert Cazimero, Melveen Leed, and Genoa Keawe; the companies of "Miss Saigon" and "Les Miserables"; and many, many others.

The gift of giving and sharing joy with people may start with Gayle's lei that they receive, but it continues as the tradition of giving is passed on by the recipients themselves – creating the most beautiful lei of all – a lei of love created by smiling faces and joyful hearts.

Pegge Hopper

"An artist whose paintings speak the beauty and serenity of the aloha spirit"

My first glimpse of Pegge Hopper was from her upstairs floor of her Nuuanu Street Chinatown Gallery, as she entered the front door cheerfully exchanging a few words with a customer who was walking out into the street at the same time. She is attractive, vivacious, and petite. I was struck by this well-known painter in Hawaii, whose portrayal of Polynesian women brought out the splendor and magnificence of their larger-than-life bodies and their natural beauty in reflective poses that could calm the restless soul.

LANAKILA
(achievement)
Ke hana maikaʻi ʻia, pono ka hoʻokāʻoi aku ʻana i ka hana.
Once we do something well, we need to figure out a way to do it better.

Pegge, a native Californian, who came to live in Hawaii in 1963, is aware of what the *aloha* spirit means and its positive power to make things better, even in paradise. She believes that it has nothing to do with religion; rather it is merely a style of behavior used by Individuals to show respect and caring for another person. In her view, it has more to do with how people feel, think, and act – their philosophical bases for what it means to be human, rather than being born into any particular culture that professes certain behaviors or unique ways of behaving. She feels that the *aloha* spirit has a universal quality – that these same behaviors exist in all people throughout the world – where they are kind, caring, and compassionate.

Pegge Hopper's paintings are loved by people throughout the world. As an islander, I truly appreciate the unique perspective she brings to the canvas of beautiful local women. I have always imagined that the island person in the painting is inviting me to visit and talk story in a comfortable and relaxing manner. Her paintings put me at ease. To explain her relationship to her work, Pegge quoted Cole Porter, who said, "My art is not my life; my life is my art." Her philosophy made me feel I was in the presence of a person who truly believed in the *aloha* spirit and understood the responsibility implied by living it.

When you step into Pegge's Nuuanu Street

Chinatown Gallery, the color, composition, drama, and beauty of her art reach out from its walls to pull you within them. But it is the individual pieces – in their diversity – that will fascinate and delight you. One cannot help but succumb to its emotion.

In listening to her journey as a full-fledged renowned artist, it seems that she is still in the process of evolving into the artist that she envisions for herself. Because she is an artist, Pegge tries to accept the beauty and ugliness of life, as well as the dark and light sides of our souls, and she has the enduring capacity to bring that alive in her art. Her ability to see things outside of their familiar context and to look behind what is, brings freshness to her paintings. She touches and speaks to many souls through her bold and brave replicas of life. It seems that her dialogue will continue to stimulate and stir more hearts as she travels further into life.

The essence of Pegge Hopper as an artist can be found in her continuous growth as a person. It was interesting to me how she goes about bringing everything into balance that is in her life – her art, her family, and friends. Pegge says she strives for balance, harmony, and enjoyment in her personal life. To do this, she looks at life as a tapestry – with beautiful colors and magnificent threads, tightly woven. Peggy believes that we weave our own tapestries – involving ourselves in work that has meaning and purpose and by helping people when we are able, rather than simply living to work. The choices we make shape our world – we have the choice of seeing the beauty that surrounds us. Our tapestries reflect the quality of our lives.

Pegge was twenty-years old when she lost her forty-five year-old mother to cancer. It made her face the reality of life – that life is fragile and tenuous--and it also made her realize how grateful she was to be alive. Pegge says that, when we are aware of the fragility of life, we tend to appreciate it when things go right. When we think this way, there is an urgency to fix things and make them right. And with that kind of mindset, she began to be grateful for life and appreciate every moment. She said that gratitude is her form of prayer – a basic element of spirituality. She believes that being grateful for life begins when we truly appreciate what we have.

Pegge feels that she has lived a charmed life and that she has been in the right place at the right time. With her work ethic, she feels she has been lucky enough to accomplish everything she has ever wanted from life. Recently, her long-time goal of building a simple, lovely home on a hillside in Honolulu has been realized. The benefits of her focused, disciplined and prolific talent that she has so generously shared with others has greatly enhanced her own life.

She shares that, along her journey in life, there is a

place that she is headed in the near future – It seems to me that Pegge's journey to that place started many moons ago. Her unique perspective paved a way into our hearts and minds – to appreciate and see the beauty that surrounds us. It is easy to project ourselves into one of her paintings – feeling the warmth and glory of life itself. Pegge Hopper has truly given the people of Hawaii – the world — a gift in and of herself –her talent to convey beauty and serenity on canvas.

Kimo Kahoano

*"He is truly an entertainer who loves people
and shows it – whether he is on or off stage.
It is simply the way he lives the aloha spirit."*

When he was born at Kapiolani Hospital, local
celebrity Kimo Kahoano made a grand entry into the
world at 10 lbs. 4 oz. – only after his mother spent 36
hours in labor. Today, Kimo still makes a huge impact
on his audiences – but he never keeps them waiting.
He's there on time with a big smile and a warm greeting. Some things do change with time.

This well-liked TV host and former radio personality
grew up in a family of six children – three boys and

three girls. He was the first boy in the family - the third in the lineup of siblings. At different times in his life, his family lived in Kalihi at the Palama Settlement Housing, Crater Road in Kaimuki and in Waimanalo. He attended Kamehameha School from grade 1 through 4 then went to Aiea Elementary and Aiea Intermediate School. He returned to Kamehameha School as a high school freshman and continued there until he graduated in 1966. As he saw it, his school experiences enhanced the quality of his life – it was exciting, interesting and fun.

At seventeen years old, he was a talented hula dancer with big dreams. In his senior year he learned a valuable lesson that would last a lifetime. A dance troupe, 'The Young Hawaiians', was being assembled at Kamehameha School to entertain in Japan. Kimo wanted to be part of that troupe and expressed a desire to try out in the audition. However, on the day of the audition, his mother asked Kimo to go with her to welcome his father, who had been away at sea on a ship for months. Kimo decided that it was far more important to go with his mother, but he knew in his heart that by doing that he had forfeited his chance to be on the troupe. When he returned to school after the auditions were completed, Kimo was surprised to learn that the coordinator of the selection process, Mr. Walter Mookini, told him that he had been chosen as an alternate because of his desire to be a part of the troupe, and his willingness to put in the time to learn the hula well. Kimo was ecstatic. Mr. Mookini, who was a teacher and a head dormitory master at the school realized how important it was to Kimo to try out for the troupe. However, he knew that Kimo had made the right choice in accompanying his mother to welcome his father back home. On retrospect, Kimo realized that Mr. Mookini, who was a talented steel guitarist and singer at the Halekulani Restaurant in Waikiki, somehow knew that Kimo needed a second chance at trying out for the show and he was able to give it to him. Of course, once Kimo learned that he was chosen as an alternate, his energies focused on doing well at the practice sessions. His progress went beyond Mr. Mookini's expectations, and when it came time to go to Japan, Kimo was included as a troupe member – he had made the cut.

The trip to Japan gave Kimo a valuable insight into the world of entertainment and how celebrities are treated --their hotel, transportation and food were provided, as well as some spending money. Kimo felt like a celebrity and he loved that feeling. He credits Mr. Mookini for giving him that opportunity to make a dream come true and to create bigger dreams for himself. Mr. Mookini had fueled the spark within Kimo for show business.

Kimo always felt comfortable in an actor's character – it was easy for him. He said it was like stepping out of his shoes into new roles that he certainly

NOKE

(commitment)

ʻO ka poʻe i ʻike i ko lākou ʻiʻini, ʻo ia nō nā poʻe e ʻapo
koke i nā mea i ʻiʻini nui ʻia i loko nō o ka noke mau.

Those who know what they want always attain their dreams much faster when they
are focused on that which they strive for in life.

enjoyed portraying. Kimo's high school experiences as a scholar and actor in the school's theatrical productions, gave him a healthy sense of accomplishment. Also, Kimo was keenly aware of his own strengths – he had a positive attitude about life, was a dreamer, an artist, and a good hula dancer. In addition, he was a very responsible person. The combination of his assets and his desire to impact the entertainment world was sure to propel him in the direction he saw for himself. He added knife dancing to his repertoire and entertained with high-profile local stars such as Danny 'Kaniela' Kaleikini, Marlene Sai, Zulu, Tommy Sands, Emma Veary, Al Harrington, Kalani Vaugh, Ed Kinney, Beverly Noa, Nina Kealiiwahamana, Jack De Mello and many others at the Hilton Hawaiian Village and the Royal Hawaiian Hotel.

In 1975, he took his infectious personality, high energy and extensive knowledge of Hawaiian music to radio. He played a wealth of Hawaiian music – much of which he handpicked on his morning show on KCCN 1420 AM. Among his favorite singers at the time were Loyal Garner, Melveen Leed, Peter Moon, the Brothers Cazimero, Cecilio and Kapono, and Mackie Feary and Kalapana. He became well-known on radio and later became a host for a 30 minute talk show on radio. Kimo said he enjoyed that experience which provided him with wonderful opportunities for personal and professional growth as he interviewed famous people such as Jay Leno, Mork Sal, Jim Nabors, and many other others who made it exciting, informative and fun.

Kimo later took his radio skills and applied them to live shows, some of which were televised. He was host of the Kodak Show in its last twelve years, has been co-host for the hula competition, 'Merry Monarch' televised program since 1981, and is in his 10th year as the TV co-host of Hawaii Stars.

Kimo is a father of three grown sons, who have been blessed with the same kind of personality and theatrical talent as their father. He remains friends with their mother, his ex-wife Lynnette Leilani Teixeria, who is a singer.

All that he has received from life Kimo continually works to give back to others. He helps in a number of charitable events, but one that he has been involved in for 25 years is the MDA Telethon. He is amazed at the amount of goodness that is in Hawaii's people. Kimo says, "Hawaii's people give way beyond their means, but not beyond their spirit." Appropriately, this year Kimo received the Moe Keale "Aloha Is" Award for Community Service at the Na Hoku Hanohano Awards. Kimo knows that although his community work has been recognized, it is his spirit of aloha that continues to uplift people's lives.

Carole Shimizu Kai Onouye

"The brilliance of this Hawaii star goes beyond her physical beauty -- it is her spirit that ignites the charitable spark within people to challenge themselves for the benefit of others."

For anyone watching Carole Kai on the *"Hawaii Stars"* stage, they might see a glamorous woman full of high energy encouraging and comforting participants on stage, and having a lot of fun bringing this exciting TV show for 10 years to its statewide viewers. But what most people don't know is that off-stage, she is an extremely generous woman, whose heart overflows with compassion when it comes to people in need. Carole has kept her focus and energies directed at making lives better through her diligent efforts throughout the years.

Carole believes that we need to always keep in focus what is really important to us. She said that her most profound lessons came from her family and they required no words – just actions. Faith, commitment, the power of love and forgiving others are immeasurable riches that Carole now shares with others.

Her physical appearance is striking – wonderful physique, with an exciting gait, tastefully glamorous in her presentation, cute dimples that gives her that childlike Shirley Temple look, and skin that belies her age. No matter what stage she is on – entertaining or raising funds for charity – Carole shares her vivacious star-studded island-grown self with the audience. She is careful to integrate the spirit of *aloha* and strives to connect with the multitude of people that surround her whenever she entertains.

Carole acknowledges that she learned early the lessons of life in her own family that helped her to make her life better. Four lessons that she never forgot was 1) you have to share what you have, 2) you have to face your problems, not run away from them, 3) be grateful for what you have and do not take things for granted, and 4) you have to have a healthy sense of humor to bear the unbearable. Her brother and sister helped her to actualize these lessons as they were growing up. Carole says that the real inspiration came from her mother Ethel, who grew up in a family of eight children. Carole shared that her maternal grandfather was a stonemason and his work can still be seen in a ono man bridge in Hanapepe and the rock walls surrounding Wheeler Army Base. Both her maternal grandparents worked extremely hard to give them a good life.

She said that when her mother's family moved from Hanapepe, Kauai to Kahalu, Oahu, they were welcomed with open arms by the Hawaiian families that lived there. There, her mother learned the secret of *aloha* – which she later imparted to Carole as the tremendous sense of giving – to share with others what you have and when you get it back be sure to pass it along, because life is a circle – it is a continuous cycle of giving and sharing.

Carole is sincere in her devotion to her God and says that life has been good to her because of the beliefs she holds about life and the people in it, which are bible-based and aimed at doing good works. Her strong belief in God and herself helped her to overcome the many obstacles she faced along her personal and professional journey. Today, she strives to have a clear conscious and do good works in the name of her Lord and feels that she can help others to come to this same serene place by praying for them.

While forgiveness may have fallen out of favor for many people, Carole is a staunch believer of it – closely tied to her religious beliefs. Carole said she built her capacity to forgive herself and others at a very early age, and that has preserved many friend-ships over the years. She believes that you must enjoy life to the fullest and when you forgive others you have more of a chance of enjoying life rather than to har-bor any negative feelings against anyone. She says the reason she forgives others is because as human beings, we all make mistakes. We must recognize our frailties and forgive others as well. This is a way of extending *aloha* to people. Carole believes that if you are willing to forgive others, perhaps when you need to be forgiven, someone else will forgive you.

As the founder of the Great *Aloha* Run, Carole has watched with delight over the years as the event invites more participants not only from Hawaii, but from abroad as well. I vividly remembered when Carole started the Carole Kai Bed Races with its whim-sical participants and the fun they were having to raise monies for charity. I could only imagine the coor-dination it took to organize such an event and the time and effort to pull it off. But she did and contin-ued her work to help other people. But what I liked about it was that she was making it fun to help others. Everyone benefited from those events.

Today, Carole keeps herself busy as the vice president and executive producer of Hawaii Stars Presents, Inc. giving her abundantly high energy towards TV productions such as Hawaii Stars & Keiki Stars, Chefs in Paradise, Golf Hawaii on TGC, "Fourth of July" at Ala Moana Center, SOS "Pride, Passion, and Dedication, "Four Strings – History of the Ukulele, and "Jan Ken Po – the Game Show". She credits her first business partner Mike McCarty for creating the concept of the Hawaii Stars and his ability to make it happen and her current partner, Dirk Fukushima for the show's on-going success.

Carole sums up her charitable work in the community by quoting Hawaii Supreme Court Justice Ronald Moon, "Public service is the rent you pay for the space you occupy on this earth." You can be sure that Carole has gone beyond her share of the rent and she continues to provide lots of opportunities for others to help too.

Danny Kaniela Kaleikini

"Hawaii's champion of the aloha spirit opens his heart to all that he meets and makes them feel he has known them for years with his contagious smile and genuinely warm greeting."

Gracious and real – two words that came into my mind as I sat with Danny 'Kaniela' Kaleikini, Mr. Aloha, at lunch. He was relaxed and looked younger than his sixty-seven years – his skin is tight and moist, and his twinkling eyes are bright and alert. But it is his beautiful smile that is infectious and never falters. He shares that with everyone who looks his way and they in turn share their smile with him.

Kaniela started to tell me of his humble beginnings in Papakolea Hawaiian Homestead near Punchbowl, and growing up in a family of ten children headed by two wonderful parents. His parents and grandparents encouraged him to sing. He began in the church choir, which peaked his interest in singing and also, stimulated his curiosity in reading the passages in the bible, It gave him a valuable insight into life and the possibilities of hope – but he never forgot the reality that it took focused and disciplined hard work to make his dreams come true. Kaniela is quick to remind those in pursuit of their dreams that "the harder you work, the luckier you will get." He knows firsthand the truism of that adage. Despite, the support he received from his family -- in particular his father -- his path to fame was not easy.

Initially, Kaniela was faced with monetary obstacles when he applied for a loan to help launch his career. A close-minded banker refused to accept his loan because he felt that all entertainers were too much of a risk in terms of borrowing money. Kaniela had a different perspective about the refusal. He assumed that the banker refused to loan him money, not because he was an aspiring entertainer – but because he was Hawaiian. Kaniela was deeply disappointed. However, he didn't dwell on this discouraging experience, instead he used it to motivate him towards the attainment of his goals. He forged ahead with confidence and the belief that he had something good to

`OLU`OLU

Kindness

Ke pā `ia ka na`au, he nāwele hemo `ole ia.

Once you touch a person's heart, you leave a lasting imprint no one else can erase.

share with others – the gift of song and *aloha* in his heart.

On April 28, 1967, he started at the Kahala Hilton and was there for over twenty-five years -- not merely entertaining Hawaii's guests and visitors --but sharing the warmth and *aloha* of our island state. Kaniela's vision of himself, his talent, personal charm, and impeccable work ethics propelled him to success and at one point in his career, he had signed a $1.5 million contract with the Kahala Hilton. The banker who refused him that initial loan must have been kicking himself in the pants.

Because of music, Kaniela could relate to various languages. He learned different languages -- Chinese, Japanese, French, and German, besides his fluency in pidgin and English -- which helped him to connect with a wider audience. Everywhere he went through-out the world – Korea, Australia, New Zealand, Hong Kong, Puerto Rico, Cuba, Japan, Europe, and Canada -- it was his goal to learn the culture and ways of its people so that he could honor and respect them in the appropriate ways. He sang, played the ukulele, nose flute, and drums for royalty, governmen-tal dignitaries, and celebrities – as well as the local citi-zens of those faraway places. His vision of spreading the *aloha* spirit became a reality with every perform-ance at the Kahala Hilton, and on every stage he per-formed on throughout the world. Today, Danny

Kaleikini is a recognized name in entertainment throughout the world, not only as a gifted entertainer who promoted Hawaii and its culture, but also as a messenger of peace and harmony through his *aloha* spirit.

Kaniela shared an article with me that he recently received. He was touched with this young man's experience at one of his performances. The article was written twenty years ago by the young man, who was on a trip to the mainland with his father. Now, almost a half century later, this same young man Chris Leong, is the Intermediate School football coach at Punahou School, where Kaniela's grandson Nicholas Hulali Kaleikini attends school. At the time he attended Kaniela's mainland performance, Coach Leong felt that Kaniela exuded *aloha* and was compelled to write the following article as a memoir. However, Kaniela never saw it until recently.

"Twenty minutes ago ended an experience that I will always remember. I sat in the audience as a spectator at the Danny Kaleikini show at Harrah's in Reno, Nevada. The feeling that I left the show with was one of pride. Mr. Kaleikini and his cast put on a marvelous performance, but the true essence of the show was Danny. His charisma sent a message to the audience that life can be one of harmony and joy. It does not matter whether that is the truth or not, but what matters is that the audience wanted to believe that it can be so. His smiling face and warmth permeated out to those sitting in the dark. As I scanned the people near to me from time to time, I could see by the expressions that they were in the land of *aloha*. Kaleikini talked of the multi-races living in one land and demonstrated by his cast the wide variety of blood that run through their veins. The songs he sang were upbeat or romantic in nature. How lucky I felt to be part of the islands. I was touched by the warmth of the show and right now I am inspired to be what Danny conveyed for an hour. I want to be a good representative of our wonderful state. I want to be warm, loving and accepting. The model of life that Danny sold for an hour is a good reminder for those of us who live in the islands. It is sad that we sometimes forget how good we have it living in paradise."

I would imagine that there are even more people like Coach Leong, who felt the glow of *aloha* in Kaniela's presence but perhaps never put it on paper and just kept it in their hearts. In 1988, Governor John Waihee, certainly recognized this quality in Kaniela and proclaimed him as the official state ambassador of *Aloha*. What a fitting tribute to a man who, as Coach Leong puts it – exudes *aloha*.

Kaniela has received numerous awards and recognitions for his charitable work in the community. Just to mention some of them, In 1971, he received the Outstanding Hawaiian of the Year Award from the

Kailua Hawaiian Civic Club; in 1978, Kaniela was admitted to the Toastmasters International Hall of Fame, receiving the Communication and Leadership Award; in 1980, he received the anuual David Malo award given by the West Honolulu Rotary Club to an outstanding Hawaiian; and in 1991 he received an honorary degree, a Doctor of Humane Letters, from the University of Hawaii at Manoa for his work in promoting the Hawaiian culture.

To give back to the community that supported and loved his work, Kaniela set up the Danny Kaleikini Foundation in the early 1980's to help community groups and students with scholarships. It is Kaniela's belief that if you want to make money personally, you need to give back to the community – because it is the people who contributed to your success. The philosophy is a long-standing island belief among locals that you need to give back to those who help to support you if you want to continue to be successful. It's a cyclical, win-win situation that Kaniela truly believes in.

When I asked how he got to be so polished as an entertainer, Kaniela said that above all he acknowledged God who has blessed him with special talents. In addition, he shared that he was a very good learner and had magnificent kumus (teachers) who helped him. Kaniela said that he watched, observed and learned how local professionals – Ray Kinney, Jimmy Kaopuiki, Hilo Hattie, Haunani Kahaleiwai and Webley

Edwards performed, and later, perfected his own style of entertainment. His attention to his work and the passion he brought to it on stage were automatically transferred to his audiences, who loved him and kept returning to his shows.

While entertainment was his primary career, Kaniela astutely positioned himself for financial security. He successfully pursed business with his wife, the former Jacqueline Wong of Tahiti, who operated their five bikini shops in Waikiki. On retrospect, one can conclude that Kaniela's trek from the Papakolea Hawaiian Homestead to owning a home in the upscale Kahala –with his own Hawaii Visitors Bureau historic marker to designate his home -- has traveled a long way, not only in terms of his financial gain, but his vast fortune in acquiring worldwide experiences and relationships.

Kaniela's insatiable appetite for fellowship and harmony keeps him focused on spreading the *aloha* spirit wherever he goes. His contagious smile is like a beacon touching faces all around him. Combined with his melodic and friendly greeting, Hawaii's Ambassador of *Aloha*, Danny Kaniela Kaleikini, continues to share the genuine spirit of *aloha* within him.

In parting, Kaniela reminds us…
Aloha is the breath of life we share with one another.
"*Aloha Ke Kahi ' i' Kahi* (Love we share with one another)
Aloha Ke Akua (God is Love)

Sol Pili Kahoʻohalahala

"A councilman, legislator and statesman whose voyage through life is navigated by the Hawaiian cultural values, concepts and practices of his kūpuna kahiko that is perpetuated in his life through his everyday interactions with those he serves."

Sol Kahoʻohalahala was born and raised on the island of Lānaʻi in a family whose lineage -- the Kamaʻuaʻua line -- goes back some 700 years. Born into a family of ten children – four boys and six girls, Sol had early lessons on how to understand and relate to other people in positive and effective ways. The collective wisdom of his *Kūkū* and *Kūpuna* were instrumental in shaping the statesman Sol is today. Their teachings were not contained in books. Their subtle knowledge, skills and wisdom were passed on in manageable portions through their words and daily actions. This has had a powerful and significant impact on Sol's life.

Sol's *kūkū* would gather for *'ohana* daily. It taught him the simple but difficult process of bringing family together at the start and end of each day with *pule (prayer)*. Sol's family looked forward to the beginning of a new day, the potential for good works and deeds as well as anticipated challenges and how to meet them. *'Ohana* has taught him this simple and important process of coming together at the start of every day to ask for guidance and later to reflect. Bringing closure at the end of the day was usually a gathering at the dinner meal where there was a lot of "talk story". If there were any problems encountered, following the mealtime, the *'ohana* would discuss it to resolve the matter and make it right. The process was used constantly to repair relationships within the family, to set things right with our surroundings and to support greater good of the community or extended family. *'Ohana* ended the evening again with *pule*.

Sol recalls the family routine that always gave you an opportunity to feel renewed with hope in the new day. This renewed hope is practiced in the concept of pono. The practice of making things right can be applied on a daily basis, with a wider audience – your extended ʻohana. It has value in establishing, maintaining and sustaining relationships.

He remembers that his father George and Uncle Sam were amazingly skilled fishermen, hunters and gatherers. They would make sure that Sol could carry and distinguish the different kind of fishing nets to use for certain fish—big-eyed nets for *kala, palani* or *enenue* and small-eyed nets for *manini, weke* or *ʻamaʻama*. Of course, Sol remembers trying to anticipate the appropriate net with identifying the fish during the tactful stalking. The innate ability of his dad and uncle has taught him to recognize and select the type of fish given the tide conditions, position of the sun and clouds and how to utilize the rippling surface of the wind. The successful catching of fish included the tedious cleaning and care of the nets well before the savoring fish could be enjoyed at a meal. It was vital to take care of the nets as an important tool to provide for the sustenance of the family. It seemed to be a chore back then for Sol, but he never forgot the routine that went with the traditions of the fishermen.

Till today, Sol remembers the procedure for taking care of the nets after their fishing trips. He said that the nets were made out of linen threads; so the first thing when they came home from fishing was to spread the nets, then clean them of all *limu* and other debris. Next, the nets were rinsed out thoroughly to get the salt water out of the linen and allowed to dry.

When the nets were thoroughly dried, they were soaked in *"shibu"* – a solution to coat the linen threads to preserve them, and lastly, the nets were hung out to dry again. Once dried, the nets were coated with a protective sheen that helped to keep them stored without damage or deterioration until the next fishing trip. This routine was repeatedly done over the years because fishing was an important means for Sol's father to provide for his large family.

You can imagine the change that Sol encountered when he was accepted as an incoming high school senior at the Kamehameha Schools. He went from a rural plantation and subsistence lifestyle to an urban 24 hour ROTC boarding school. Sol describes himself as the "Gomer Pyle" in rifle marching formations, turning right when everyone turned left. At home on Lāna'i, a rifle was used for hunting and not for parades. Following a successful year and graduation at the Kamehameha Schools in 1969, Sol went back to Lāna'i immediately to plan, organize and decorate the commencement gymnasium in preparation for the ceremonies of his lifelong classmates at the Lāna'i High School. Sol wanted to be sure that he supported and fulfilled some of his responsibilities to his classmates on Lāna'i even though he had been gone for their last school year together. That summer they all worked in the pineapple fields one last time. Sol remembers how difficult it was to bring that summer to an end before they would part ways, each setting out

PO'OKELA

(excellence)

Ahuwale ka po'okela i kāu hana iā ha'i.

It is through the way you serve others that your greatness will be felt.

on their life's journey. It would be rare that he would see his classmates during the next five years as he attended college on the mainland.

In 1974, Sol would return to Lāna'i to prepare for his wedding to his college sweetheart, Lynn Humphrey. That summer, they would marry on the beautiful bay at Napili, Maui. Soon after, Sol and Lynn would move back to Lāna'i where they would spend the next twenty-five years to make it their home. It was here on Lāna'i that they would raise their four daughters, Kōleka, Pualani, Ha'aheoikana'auaoonakeiki-maika'iāmekaponooka'āina'oLāna'i and Kai'olu, along with their four horses, two dogs, five chickens, three ducks and two guinea pigs. It was a place where they continued their cultural practices with their 'ohana; fishing, hunting, gathering, camping, hiking, horseback riding, singing, chanting and dancing hula, and spending time with na Kūpuna. It was time spent rediscovering the natural and cultural history of Lāna'i, its flora and fauna, its places and their names, and the mo'olelo. Sol and his 'ohana feel privileged to have been steeped in the true Lāna'i island "sense of place".

During those years, Lynn was a schoolteacher, homemaker and mother. Sol would begin his work career with the State Department of Agriculture, a paralegal for the Legal Aid Society of Hawai'i, physician assistant a the Lāna'i Family Health Center, preschool teacher at E Mālama ina Keiki o Lāna`i Preschool and the Assistant Manager of Hotel Lāna`i. Eventually, Sol became the General Manager in the last four years of his tenure at Hotel Lāna`i. In 1989, Sol became the Director of Cultural Resources at the Lodge at Kō`ele and the Mānele Bay Hotel until 2003. In his capacity, Sol was able to implement the management by "Aloha" program integrating a Lāna`i sense of place, sharing the history and culture of Lāna`i with the employees and guests, conducted familiarity tours throughout Lāna`i to help the employees to incorporate the concepts of aloha – caring, respect, kindness and support — in their customer care programs. Having met George Kanahele, a training and management consultant, Sol was convinced that working to instill the genuine experience of aloha through a rediscovery of ones roots, convinced the Human Resources Director at the Lodge at Kō`ele to integrate and incorporated the values of the Hawaiian culture. It was an opportunity to perpetuate the aloha spirit in the hotel industry on Lāna`i.

In 1975 Sol's interest in rediscovering his Hawaiian and Polynesian roots lead him to the crew deck of Hōkūle`a, the 62-foot double-hulled Hawaiian voyaging canoe. His intrigue with the wa`a kaulua and his persistence afforded him the opportunity of a lifetime to train on the island of Moloka`i where he made his first interisland voyage on the Hōkūle`a from Moloka`i to O`ahu. Sol never forgot the awe inspired spirit of

the canoe that chilled his spine as they surfed fifteen-
foot swells with winds gusting to 30 knots in the Ka'iwi
channel crossing. He recalls standing on the deck,
drenched in sea spray, both arms stretched out with
hands clenching the rails, sails billowing with wind,
Hōkūle'a in flight; it was incredible to understand the
swiftness of the canoe that was skillfully lashed with
cordage, using no nuts or bolts. The canoe was an old
Polynesian design, beautiful, seaworthy, and highly
efficient on the ocean under wind. It was at that very
moment that the revelation of his being, his belonging
and his birthright connection to his Hawaiian-
Polynesian roots were made clear and evident. After
many years of interisland sailing voyages, Sol was invited in1987 to become a crewmember on the "Voyage
of Rediscovery". It was his first opportunity to sail in the
South Pacific from Tahiti to the Marquesas; Sol would
never forget the warmth and ho'okipa shared by the
people. It reminded him of his 'ohana and he felt at
home. In 1992, Sol was a crewmember on the voyage
called "No Na Mamo" a voyage for the children from
Tahiti to Ra'iatea and on to Rarotonga, Cooke Islands
for the Pacific Arts Festival. Later in 1998, Sol was privileged to join the crew of Hōkūle'a as she concluded
her most challenging voyage to link the Polynesian triangle with Rapanui. Sol shared that his experiences of
traveling across the Pacific Ocean in this double-
hulled sailing canoe has filled him with a spirit of
adventure, a sense of pride and genuine accomplishment and a sense of identity as a Hawaiian – and his

link to the greater islands of the Pacific and the Polynesian Triangle and its people.

In 1976, Sol met Moloka`i visionary, George Helm. At a meeting on Moloka`i, Sol was inspired by the wisdom and passion that George exuded for *"Aloha `āina"*. The concept of love for the land would become a lifetime commitment to stop the bombing of the island of Kaho`olawe by the U.S. Navy and to return to island to people of Hawai`i. Sol recounts the joining of hands from all parts of Hawai`i nei, united in one purpose, to demonstrate that love for one's land is far greater and more important than the desecration of land that sustains and feeds us. This thirty year movement would culminate in the loss of George Helm and Kimo Mitchell at sea, the stopping of the bombing of Kaho`olawe, the return of the island to people of Hawai`i and the restoration of the island for its eventual return to a sovereign Hawaiian Entity. Sol is reminded once more of the teaching of *na kūpuna* and the importance of balance, care and respect for who we are as people and for the islands in this place that we call home.

This soft-spoken, humble man relates to the concept and practice, *"I ka wā mamua, I ka wā mahope"*; in order for one to move forward, one must look to the past. Through the many stories of his *kūkū*, Sol has been able to bridge the past to the present and has demonstrated a calm wisdom as an effective leader

to take us into the future. He works endlessly to preserve the Hawaiian culture and its values, while helping others to understand the importance of these values in our modern contemporary world through his
own community involvement and actions in the politi-
cal arena. Sol has served as an outstanding member
of the Maui County Council representing the island of
Lāna'i, and a leader in the Hawai'i State House of
Representatives, representing the islands of: Moloka'i,
Lāna'i, East Maui, Kaho'olawe, Molokini and
Kalaupapa. It is the only district that represents islands
in the state of Hawai'i, known collectively as "Maui Nui
A Kama", the greater islands of Kamalalawalu. Sol has
dedicated a part of his life's work to representing the
needs of its people, both common and diverse. His
mission is to help the people he serves, and to preserve the culture and values that make Hawai'i a
unique place to live.

Sol reflects on his life's journey as somewhat like the
navigation of a voyaging canoe as it weaves through
the challenging seas and the winds of change. It is
key that you understand and utilize to the best advantage the conditions presented to you if you want ultimately to determine the outcome, quality and success of your voyage. Sol understands that in his journey through life it is important to steer a course that
has been seasoned with knowledge, experience, trust,
and a keen sense of self. Embracing the values, experiences, knowledge and skills taught by na kūpuna

kahiko and apply the best information and assessment of the conditions that surround us today, there is no challenge that cannot be met. By implementing these practices today with our *keiki,* we bring honor to our ancestors.

Sol continues on his life's journey to adopt the practices of his *kūkū* and *na kūpuna* that are in keeping with the traditional Hawaiian values of aloha. It is a lifelong journey that focuses on raising people's consciousness about respect for oneself, others and our precious environment. It is in his gift of sharing the best of himself with others that Sol helps others to give their best.

John Keawe

" *A Grammy Award winning slack-key guitarist, song-writer and vocalist who treasures what he has learned from those who have come before him, and skillfully weaves that into the gift he continually shares with others -- his own style of contemporary music that speaks of love – of life, ohana and homeland.*"

One day as I was working in our store, Successories of Hawaii, I began talking about inspirational people within the State of Hawaii with one of our customers, Rick Eveleth from Waimea. At one point, he shared the name of a musician who lived on the Big Island, whose slack-key guitar music and songs touched people's hearts. I had never heard of the musician before this discussion with Rick. The next day Rick dropped off some informational materials on the musician at the store. My curiosity lead to me to run into Borders Bookstore next door to our store, and get the musician's current CD, "*Aloha Kaikua'an*", packed with wonderful slack key guitar instrumentals. I was so impressed with his music that I played it repeatedly at the store for all our customers to hear. After listening to his music, I was compelled to call him so I could include his story in this book. That was the first time I talked with John Keawe,

My first impression was that John was a very courteous, kind and generous person. After sharing some information about myself, and the book I was writing, John agreed to be part of it. On our next phone call a couple of days later, John shared how he began to play slack key music, write songs, and sing his original compositions. Because he knew I only had the CD with the instrumentals on it, he promised to send me three of his earlier CD's in which he sings and plays a variety of songs. Within the next few days, I received three of his CD's -- "*Keaweualani*", "*Heartfelt*" and "*Christmas is...*"in the mail. Listening to them took me on a musical journey deep within my heart – touching familiar emotions of life in this wonderful place that we live.

John's gift to all those who hear his music is his songs, which speak of love – of life, ohana, and homeland. It is in his courage to be open and honest with his words and feelings that give wings to his songs. His music easily takes you from where you are in your sometimes fast-paced world to where you really want to be – in a peaceful place surrounded by beauty, serenity and love. Not every musician can take you to that precious comfortable place.

Four slack-key masters – legendary Gabby Pahanui, Leonard Kwon, Raymond Kane, and Keola Beamer influenced John's musical compositions as he struggled to learn how they made the sounds of the slack-key music. However, it was the well-known contemporary slack-key guitarist and songwriter, Keola Beamer, who inspired John to create musical pieces of his own and write songs about things and people that touched his emotions. His eventual meeting with Keola Beamer led to an invitation to Mr. Beamer's *Aloha* Camp on the Big Island, in which attendees learn to hula and to play the ukulele and the slack-key guitar. Next year John takes his music to a broader audience as he tours the United States with Keola Beamer. The tour will start in the East Coast then continue across country all the way to the West Coast. John is excited about going on that tour because it will be his first trip to the East Coast.

When I asked John how he got started in the music business, he said that in 1978, he sent in a cassette tape of his song, *Ka'auhuhu Homestead*, to a radio

WAIWAI

Prosperity

`O ke ana waiwai, he mea kālā `ole. `O ia ho'I ka waiwai maoli.

To measure wealth, look around you at the things money cannot buy.

That is your true fortune.

station on Oahu for a song contest that they were sponsoring statewide. John's song was selected as part of the twelve winning songs and the radio station eventually produced an album of the 12 selected songs, which they played continuously on their station. The exposure to John's song statewide gave him the confidence to write and sing more songs.

One of John's songs I particularly liked was "*Tutu's Slack Key*", which John wrote as a tribute to his grand-fathers, Joseph Keaweualani and John Coit, who encouraged and inspired him to play slack-key music.

When I was just a little boy my tutu said to me
Do me one favor and in your life time learn to
play slack key

But I grew up with other things – thought I had
lots of time
To live and learn and laugh and play – in the
bright sunshine

But tutu was a stubborn man and he kept
after me
To sit and listen and watch his fingers as he
played his slack key

Tutu loved his music – one thing he asked
of me

*Learn the beauty of the music – the beauty of
slack key*

*Then Uncle Sam took me away for an eternity
Through four long years I learned to play – my
tutu's style
Slack key*

*When I returned tutu was dying and he could
hardly speak
But he passed away with a peaceful smile
when he heard me
Play slack key*

*Tutu loved his music – one thing he asked
of me
Learn the beauty of the music – the beauty of
slack key.*

I'm glad that Rick Eveleth came into our store that day and introduced me to John Keawe – a living treasure of *aloha*. Certainly, our lives can only be made better by John, and people like Rick, whose recognition of *aloha* and sharing of this goodness with others, can hopefully perpetuate this wonderful feeling of the *aloha* spirit.

Maryanne Kusaka

"She has an indomitable spirit of aloha that never falters – no matter what the situation, and through her example, many people have come to understand the importance of positive actions -- both personally and as a community—as expressions of aloha. "

In whatever role she takes – as a friend, politician or concerned citizen – Maryanne goes beyond caring by taking action to make things better than it was before. As the former mayor of Kauai, Maryanne Kusaka made it a point to put the *aloha* spirit into a credo that helped to guide and inspire her leadership team in their work. It is evident that what she truly believes in – the spirit of the people – has motivated her to create a sense of community pride and unity in its people.

Anyone visiting the island can notice the impact that Maryanne and her leadership team had made on Kauai. It was during her administration as mayor that many beautification projects, including the well-manicured and welcoming gateway to Kauai (the entry and exit areas of the airport) took place. When you travel to Kauai, you can instantly notice the difference there is in the ambience of Kauai – it seems more friendly and welcoming. It is the legacy that Maryanne has left on the island – the lingering spirit of *aloha* -- she simply made a huge difference to Kauai and its people as mayor.

No matter where you meet Maryanne, you will notice a very dignified, perfectly attired, and well-behaved individual. She has the humbleness of a spiritual leader and the strength of a world leader. Her presence is a comfortable, but commanding one – people pay attention to what she has to say. As a former teacher for 33 years, Maryanne always used her power to influence and inspire her students and their parents through her goodness and sincere efforts. They fully appreciated having an educator who responded to their needs and wanted the best for their children.

As the former mayor of Kauai County, Maryanne's leadership in the recovery from Hurricane Iniki in 1992

was highly acknowledged by Kauai's people. The huge setbacks of that tragedy and the devastation that it brought to the residents were tremendous. When she became mayor in 1994, her passion for restoring a sense of community pride and volunteerism gave the people of Kauai the spirit they needed to meet the challenging economic period they faced. But even through that difficult time, Maryanne was quick to point out that there was a positive outcome to the tragedy. It brought its citizens closer together as a community. She said that as she traveled from town to town after the Hurricane hit, she noticed that because everyone faced similar conditions – without running water or electricity – they bonded together closer to help one another.

Food from neighbor's freezers were brought out for everyone to eat and community barbeques became a common sight. It was a heart-warming feeling that lasted beyond the recovery period. As mayor she put her heart and soul into restoring to the people the life they had enjoyed before the hurricane. Today, many visitors 'feel' the *aloha* spirit on Kauai where neighbors help one another and share with strangers. It's a good feeling.

As a community service advocate she continues to give back to the people. *Aloha* has always had a special meaning for Maryanne. It is simply the way she lives. She loves people and keeps them in focus in whatever she is doing. She does not ask of anyone what she cannot deliver herself. And with her tremendous reserve of *aloha*, she forges ahead to make things better for others. That is her way of saying I care – by doing what is in her heart and giving her precious gift of *aloha*.

Perhaps her family upbringing was what influenced her in that direction. Maryanne says that her mother, Mary Pino, who was the chief operator for the Hawaiian Telephone Company in Hana, was 'full of *aloha*'. Their home was the social magnet of the community and her mother welcomed all who stopped there on their way out of Hana. There were many parties with lots of singing and playing of music. Around dinnertime, the house would be full of people sampling her mother's famous chicken hekka and portuguese soup. These activities certainly helped her to become the gracious hostess that she is known to be at home and in the community. Oftentimes her mother asked her to baby-sit the children, whose parents partied at their home. Her experiences with the children gave her a deeper appreciation and enjoyment of them. Later, her mother would encourage her to go into teaching because she was keenly aware of how Maryanne loved children and more importantly, how they responded to her.

Maryanne loves bringing people together -- she says it is in her inclusion nature -- and is credited for creating partnerships that helped to achieve shared goals. As mayor, she reactivated a partnership with Ishigaki City, Kauai's sister city in Okinawa, becoming the first mayor to visit the Japanese city and was the force in the continuance of that program. Another partnership that is on-going after seven years, is the student exchange program involving nearly 80 high school students and 5 or 6 teachers, from Oshima Island in the Yamaguchi Prefecture. The students are partnered with a local high school and live with local families for four days. The exchange program fosters an awareness of the Hawaiian culture, the English language, high school and family life on Kauai. In addition, there is a continuing exchange program for students, which is sponsored by the Rotary Club of Kauai and supported by the county, which provides students an insight into the culture and language of Japan.

During her term as mayor, Maryanne and her leadership team worked diligently with the American Society of Travel Agents (ASTA) to bring 650 travel agents and owners of travel agencies to Kauai so that they could be see firsthand that the island was repaired and open for business after the devastation caused by Hurricane Iniki. Their support and efforts helped to get tourists to visit the island once again, and helped to jumpstart the economy and lower the unemployment rates on Kauai.

In 1996, she started the Ambassador of *Aloha*

KIAMANAʻO

(focus)

ʻO ka hele ʻana ma hoʻokahi ala me ka ʻauana ʻole ka
hana no ka loaʻa ʻana i kou ʻiʻini. E hāpai ʻoe i ke kiamanaʻo ma mua ou, a na ke kiamanaʻo e alakaʻi iā ʻoe.

To tread the main point and never swerve from it, is the surest way to get what you
want in life. Focus on what you want, and what you focus on you will get.

Program for children as a private, non-profit scholar-ship program for kids interested in the culture and the arts. Children's lives have been enhanced because of the monies they have been given to experience activ-ities and events outside of Kauai. Maryanne says that they remind recipients of the scholarship funds that as they travel outside of Kauai they must be mindful of their behavior and share the spirit of *aloha*, because while people may forget their names, they will always remember where they came from, and it will be a reflection on the people of Kauai.

On a personal note, it is said that her yard is like a magnificent garden – beautiful plants grow there. Maryanne is especially proud of her orchids, which she says are good to her – they keep blooming and she keeps taking the blossoms to special events in town. Also, she loved to free-dive with her husband and his friends as they dived for lobster, squid and kumu. She often took the courageous role of holding the string of fish that they speared, and had to be on the constant alert for sharks that wanted a taste of the catch. Her love of diving and fishing prompted her to educate others to the care of the ocean resources and the respect that is due them.

Maryanne was born in Kamuela on the Big Island and raised on Maui – in the peaceful and serene set-ting of Hana. She attended high school on Oahu at Mid-Pacific Institute and graduated from the University of Northern Colorado with a bachelor's degree in elementary education. She is a person who blooms where she is planted, and Kauai has been truly fortunate to have a woman who, as an educator and mayor has influenced their lives in so many positive ways.

As you leave Kauai, you will notice a sign affixed on a lava wall to the left of the entry to the airport, which was erected during her term as mayor. It reads, "*Mahalo*! (Thank you!) Until we meet again." As Maryanne sees it, the *aloha* spirit is an enduring one that goes full circle. It never ends, not even on parting. It is the spirit of *aloha* that stays within all who has felt it – no matter where they go.

Melveen Leed

"She is one of Hawaii's brightest and longest-lasting stars in the galaxy of homegrown talent. She brings laughter and high-quality music wherever she entertains as she belts out her tunes – which range from Hawaiian slack-key music to Nashville-type local country music. And yet, although her journey into music brought her fame, glamour, and lots of publicity, her wholesome and down-to-earth personality makes you feel like she's the girl next door."

While entertaining in the Showroom at the Ala Moana Hotel in 1979, Melveen started what she called, "The Love Phone Connection." While on stage, she would call terminally ill cancer patients, children as well as adults, whose first names were provided by people in the audience. The audience would say a big hello to the patients, and then Melveen would sing for them. Oftentimes, she would visit the patients the next day so she could meet them in person and take a little gift for them. That was her way of extending her *aloha*.

One day, while we were having lunch at the Oahu Country Club, I received a call from one of my friends, Sharon Hicks. Sharon and Bobby Takei were organizing a birthday party for Francois Wallace, who was fighting cancer, and Sharon called to see if I would be there. I told her I would and hung up. I shared with Melveen what a good thing Sharon and Bobby were doing by inviting all of Francois' friends to help celebrate his 64th birthday. Instantly she asked, "When is his birthday party?" I told her that I thought it was on the 26th of September. Melveen reached for her palm pilot to check her calendar. Then she asked, "Do you want me to sing at his party? I can do that – for free." I was stunned. Here was this extremely busy entertainer who was offering to sing at a stranger's birthday party. I said, "Of course! I'm sure Francois would love it." So I called Sharon back and she was elated. However, when Sharon said that the party would be on the 25th of September, Melveen was disappointed. She would be on Maui judging a falsetto contest on that date. However, she asked for Francois' birth date and phone number. "I'll call him on his birthday and sing for him," Melveen said. Sharon thanked her, and Melveen put the information in her palm pilot. I was impressed and told her what a nice thing it was for her to do that for Francois. Melveen said, "I wanted to do that!"

Melveen Leed was born in 1943 and raised on Molokai until 1959 when she moved to Honolulu. Currently she lives on Oahu but makes frequent visits to her home island to visit family and entertain for charitable events there. During her early years, one person who made a permanent impression on her and whom she calls "the pillar of my life" was her grandfather, William Ellsworth Place, who was of English, German, and Hawaiian ancestry. He instilled in her good moral standards and taught her that "where God resides, don't violate it" – that the land and its people are to be honored and respected. He was a self-taught mechanic who worked for Maui County, and literally lived off the land by fishing, hunting for deer and wild pig, and raising livestock. He was especially good at mending fishnets, and although he never taught her how to do that, Melveen watched him with interest. She never realized that years later she would find herself mending a huge fish net in Tahiti.

At the time, Melveen was married to a Tahitian male who worked on Aratika, one of the Fuamotu islands in the Tahitian Atoll. She lived on Aratika for one year, and her description of the island was heavenly – with

the beauty, peace and serenity, which people continually seek for their ultimate happiness. She loved living
there and often went free diving and fishing in the
waters off the island.

One day, a huge foreign ship sailed into the waters
of Aratika with a large drag net for catching fish.
Melveen's husband and the other islanders asked the
foreigners to leave immediately and gave them an
ultimatum if they didn't. The foreigners quickly threw
their net overboard and immediately departed. The
islanders retrieved the huge net and used it to catch
black-striped *Ulua*. However, over time, the net had a
lot of large holes in it from sharks getting into the nets
in chase of the Ulua catch. Melveen's husband and
the others brought the torn net to shore and hung it on
several coconut trees to see the extent of the damage and determine how they could mend the net.
Melveen examined the net, closed her eyes, and saw
a vision of how she could mend it. She then took the
hi'a (needle) and *aho* (string) in her hand and told the
others that she would mend the net. She quickly went
about doing just that – knot by knot. It was as if her
grandfather was guiding her hands as she knotted
and connected each segment until the net was com-
pletely mended.

Melveen's get-up-and-go philosophy in life has lead to
live performances on stage both here and abroad in
many different countries. She also has 20 recordings

to her credit, including one, which she recently recorded in Nashville, Tennessee. In addition, Melveen is a pen and ink artist, and also designs jewelry and pareau. Her latest venture is her new perfume line called, "Manoa". Additionally, Melveen is writing her autobiography and has written a children's story that she read to students at Royal Elementary School as part of the "Read To Me" program sponsored by the Rotary Club of Honolulu Sunrise, of which Melveen is an honorary member.

Within the past three years, Melveen was hospitalized twice for heart complications. She experienced the first of these life-threatening situations at the funeral of her long-time friend Loyal Garner and the second after her performance aboard a cruise liner. However, today she is diligent about taking her medication, and she watches her diet and activities more carefully. But it hasn't stopped her from giving of herself. She is still a beautiful and top-notch entertainer who maintains a positive outlook of life and whose spirit touches many people. As a songstress extraordinaire, she knows that the show must go on – and she is certainly doing just that.

Marie Nakanishi Milks

*"She is considered a good listener, not only because
she carefully listens to people but because they
know she is listening to them with her heart
– it is evident in her words and actions."*

The former Oahu Circuit Court Judge Marie Milks
had spent her entire judicial career carefully listening
to other people in a court of law. During her 24 years
on the bench, she had to be tough, decisive, quick-
witted and fair. Lawyers who worked with her had a
high regard for her professionalism --- always prepared
for her cases, willing to listen to all arguments without
prejudging the case, and her consistent approach to

the law with great intellect. Marie handled many high profile cases during her time on the bench, including the largest criminal trial in the last 50 years in the state of Hawaii – the multiple-murder trial of Xerox copy machine repairman Byran Uyesugi. Her commendable performance in court over the years was a great testimony to her appointment in 1984 as the first female judge to the Circuit Court.

Her dynamic personality attracts people to her company – she is fun, intelligent, and down-to-earth. And yet, when you get to know her, you see in this very confident and secure woman, a shyness and innocence that is pleasantly refreshing. One day last December, Marie came excitedly into our store at Ward Centre and shared that she had just given a friend the best Christmas gift that she could think of. I was curious. I wanted her to describe the gift. She began with a story. This person was experiencing such a difficult time as she tried to make sense of some of the things that were happening in her life. After listening to her, Marie made a decision to give the best gift that she could think of – a gift of listening. She told her friend that she would be there for her as a listener no matter what time of the day or night that she needed to talk. Wow! I thought, what a valuable gift. Everyone would love to have a gift like that.

I can remember when my husband and I were invited to the Milks' home to have dinner with them on a

HOʻOKAULIKE

(equality)

ʻO ka hoʻokaulike, ke hoʻokaulike i nā mea a pau
i loko o ke ola, Loaʻa ka lōkahi me ka maluhia.

When you bring into balance all that is in
your life, you will find harmony and peace.

Friday evening. When we arrived, Marie was busily preparing dinner, while Bill graciously welcomed all four of us dinner guests. They were such a good team – he was a perfect host introducing everyone and showing us around the place with interesting things to share about the house itself. When we were summoned to the dinner table, we all sat comfortably around the table with the culinary delights Marie had prepared for us. Everything was so tastefully presented and the foods were scrumptious. I was so impressed that Marie was able to get everything together after working till late afternoon that day. She was so relaxed, cheerful and interested as the conversation moved from one subject to another. Amazing, I thought to myself – to have this extremely busy woman with such a demanding job not only to take time out to cook for her guests at the week's end, but also to create a wonderful ambience in which her guests felt at home in their pleasant and peaceful abode. I knew that I was in the presence of an extraordinarily gifted woman –truly centered and balanced in her life.

Marie is a world traveler, who enjoys taking some of her friends along on her trips so they can share the excitement in the culture, language and people of the country. She has been to various places in Europe, Asia, and various places in the Continental United States. In the past two months, Marie has been on two different trips -- she traveled with some friends to Southern Peru to visit Machu Picchu—the ruins of a large ancient Inca city in the Andes in September, and in October visited Japan with her husband Bill.

I especially loved hearing about Marie's upbringing and the lessons that her parents passed on to her. Marie shared how her mother was so intent in having Marie do well in her studies that she would go to the River Street area in downtown Honolulu to a used book shop there and purchase older copies of The National Geographic for a nickel or a dime. Marie loved the magazines. Besides reading about the interesting places and its people in the magazine, it had wonderful pictures for Marie to cut out for her school projects. Marie always appreciated her mother's concern for her children's education and her efforts to help them.

Marie was always concerned about her mother's welfare -- especially after her father died. One day, Marie shared that her mother was catching the bus every morning from the McCully area to downtown Honolulu to have breakfast at Mc Donald's Restaurant with some of her friends. She enjoyed their company and made it a daily routine. That made Marie happy – that her mother was so independent and taking charge of her life. However, as time passed, her aunt told Marie that she had seen her mother sharing a cup of coffee with an elderly gentleman at the McDonald's restaurant in downtown Honolulu. It peaked Marie's curiosity.

When Marie asked her mother about that, she matter-of-factly told Marie that they were sharing the cost of the coffee – no more, no less – because if you paid for one cup of coffee, the refills would be free. Marie just laughed and thought it was so funny.

Marie's sense of humor is delightful. When you're around her, you're bound to break out in giggles or a burst of laughter. One evening as we talked on the phone, she mentioned to me that she had just received a thank you card from a friend who accompanied her on a trip. The friend wrote to thank Marie for the wonderful time that she had on the trip and especially to thank her for helping her to remember how to have fun. I guess like so many of us, we sometimes need to forget how to work and remember how to play to enjoy life to the fullest.

It is said that hearing is a gift, while listening is a skill. And people who know Marie would attest to her ability to not only listen with genuine interest, but to also ask the right questions that make you feel she cares about you. It becomes a gift to the other person. Everybody loves to be in the company of an active listener, but it is a rare occasion to find a truly compassionate person who is willing to accept you for who you are, spend time hearing what you have to say, and inviting you to share more about yourself. Not everyone is gifted enough to do this successfully. Marie has certainly demonstrated that she is.

Robert "Barefoot Bob" Morrison

"As an artist, his hands give the aloha that is in his heart. His hands translate the beauty that he sees in the coconut tree and other people see it in his basket weaving and paintings – it is his gift of aloha."

On a sunshiny Saturday morning in September, as I rushed over to the Neal Blaisdell Arena for an hour of book signing at a Women's Exposition, I certainly didn't expect to find a very interesting author sitting next to me creating the stuff that he wrote about. It was such a pleasant experience, because Robert Morrison is just that kind of guy – easy to get to know and quite nice. And although it was our first meeting, I felt I knew him for a long time.

There were three of us Island Heritage authors scheduled for the same time slot that day – it was a new experience for me to be paired with two other authors. I was unfamiliar with both of them. However, Robert appeared friendly and started to talk to me as soon as I sat down. He continued to work on his weaving as I watched him take the sturdy yellow-tipped waxy green coconut fronds and weave them into sturdy baskets that has made him so well-known among the island people. For me, it was incredible seeing this blue-eyed, long sand-colored hair tied in a ponytail -- sort of a Willie Nelson type of a fellow, taking coconut fronds and weaving absolutely gorgeous baskets out of them. He took his work seriously and focused on what he was doing, but he was gracious and courteous in his conversation with me as he continued with his weaving. His talent awed me, but I was mesmerized by the kind of person that he was – kind, humble, talented, open and honest.

As I flipped through his beautifully illustrated book, I saw that he had made some of the same baskets at the book signing session that were shown in the book. "Wow! This is great, I thought – here's somebody who writes about weaving baskets and can actually make them the way it's shown in the book. He certainly walks the talk" As an observer, you could see that he

enjoyed the whole process of weaving and his creation was an outcome of his enjoyment.   You could
see and feel his passion for weaving in the way he
went about creating the baskets.

I asked him how he got started weaving baskets.
His spontaneous response was simple. Robert shared
that when he was a kid, he loved to watch war
movies. And when there were war movies that took
place in the Pacific, his attention would never go to
the action of the characters, it was always focused on
the background of the particular Pacific Island – the
tropical scenery (which he now paints). In particular,
his attention would always go to the coconut trees.
Robert said that even as a young man when he went
on a trip to Tahiti and rode around the island on a
moped, he would stop and watch the palm trees,
which fascinated him.

Robert shared that when he was eight-years old he
came on a trip to Hawaii with his parents, who lived in
Seal Beach, California near Huntington Beach.   The
moment he stepped off the plane, Robert shared that
he could feel that this was definitely where he
belonged.

On that same trip, he met a man that would
change his life. Uncle Harry was a Hawaiian man who
weaved coconut fronds at the Hilton Hawaiian Village.
Robert would stop and watch Uncle Harry weave.

Robert often asked Uncle Harry to teach him to weave, but his request always fell on deaf ears. Eventually though, Uncle Harry realized that Robert was serious about learning so he asked Robert to sit down besides him, while he taught the young boy how to weave. A willing and interested student, Robert watched, listened intently and eventually learned how to weave coconut fronds at the tender age of eight years old. After several vacation trips to Hawaii, Robert returned in the 1970's to make Hawaii his permanent home. He currently lives in Waikane, Oahu, and has no intention of leaving this peaceful place. It is interesting to note that Robert continued to learn and work with Uncle Harry until just a few years ago when Uncle Harry had a stroke.

However, it was well into his adult life when he started weaving baskets as a art. One day while at Sunset Beach, he was weaving his coconut frond baskets when a young local boy came up to him and asked him, "What kind of leaves are you weaving?" Robert was surprised and disappointed that the young man did not even realize that the fronds that he was weaving came from the coconut tree, which is abundant throughout the Hawaiian islands. Robert thought, "What a shame, so much culture is lost when the young people are not made aware of their heritage and the things that surround them. For Robert, the coconut tree was the tree of life. All that a person needed to survive in life could be found in a coconut

MINOʻAKA

(smile)

ʻO ka minoʻaka, he minoʻaka like kākou ma ka
ʻōlelo like. He ʻōlelo maopopo leʻa ka minoʻaka.

We all smile in the same language. Smiling is a universal language.

tree – food, shelter, water, clothing, liquor, etc. He also saw beauty in the tree and wanted to make beautiful things from it. Robert wanted to share those concepts with more people, so he started to weave in the public arena and share his art with a broader audience. He says that weaving is fun – and the best part is that it is free! Anyone can do it, if they are willing to learn.

Sadly, when Robert wanted to learn other techniques of weaving, no one wanted to share those techniques with him. So he built his style of weaving upon what he learned from Uncle Harry and from other techniques such as the layered weaving that he learned in Thailand. Unlike the people he approached that were unwillingly to share their talent, Robert encourages people to come by his place on Saturdays to learn this art. He even teaches a class on weaving at the Windward Community School for Adults at the Kalaheo High School on Wednesday nights and wrote a book, "The Guide to Basket Weaving" to teach others the art of weaving coconut fronds and pass on the skills and knowledge he had acquired about weaving.

Education has always played a big part in Robert's life. The culture and talents of the people of Hawaii is important to Robert. Several years back, Robert helped get funding through a grant to help people in communities such as Nanakuli and Waianae on the island of Oahu, to market their products, pass on their culture and make money, while sharing these valuable aspects of our Hawaii way of life. He said that many people in these communities didn't realize that they had valuable talents – this was a way to bring it out and share it with others. Robert says, "That's what it is all about – sharing what we know and love. What good is it if you can't share it or you don't have anybody to share it with? I think that's happiness – isn't it?"

A man of *aloha* like Robert had a definite place in this book. He lives the *aloha* spirit, values it and shares it on a continuous basis. It is his way of life. At our Saturday book signing session, Robert was unpretentious and upfront as he shared stories of his life with me over a bowl of chili and rice. I felt honored that he had disclosed such personal tidbits about his life and his professional career as a weaver and painter. He is certainly a person who when he sees beauty can translate that into tangible artistic pieces so that others can appreciate that beauty as well. That's a real talent. It takes heart to do that!

Allan Silva

"He stands tall. While his height might impress you on first glance -- it is in his steadfast belief in Hawaii's youth and his tireless efforts to inspire them to take charge of their lives that leaves a lasting impression."

When Allan Silva walks into a room people notice him. He is a tall (6"7" ft.), handsome, and a personable guy, whose smile lights up a room. Those who surround him can certainly feel his gentle, humble and respectful nature. His physical presence signals to others that he is a person who sincerely cares about people and enjoys his interactions with them.

Because of his physical appearance, Allan has been likened to Tony Robbins, the well-known motivational speaker, which he considers a compliment. But those who know Allan say that he has established his own image and popularity as Hawaii's exciting inspirational speaker for youth. He sets his own pace and is fueled by his passion to uplift students' spirit so they can pursue their life's dream. Student assemblies are just 'a piece of cake' for Allan. In those huge crowds, he conveys important messages of hope, love and caring for each other. To date, he has worked with more than 40,000 students each year in Hawaii and throughout the United States.

The former high school and college basketball coach is busily paving his professional path by continuously conducting pep talks that help to inspire and educate elementary and middle school students. Oftentimes, the topic that he shares with kids is about the *aloha* spirit -- it's meaning and how they can give this feeling to others. He helps them to develop a positive vision of themselves and then helps them to set goals to actualize that vision. Allan says that he loves working with youngsters and adults.

Of Portuguese and Hawaiian heritage, Allan is proud of his lineage. He considers himself fortunate to have been blessed with great parents and grandparents, who helped to instill in him, the traditional values of caring, sharing and loving. Words of wisdom from his dad and his grandmother, who spoke fluent Hawaiian, shared with him the importance of learning and living the *aloha* spirit. Allan says that he can still hear his grandmother's advice, "Allan, always remember *aloha*. Treat people with *aloha*, because the way you treat them will be felt forever. They may not remember all that you tell them, but they will always remember how you treated them. So treat them nice." This is a lesson that Allan always remembered. It is the credo that he lives by which gives him great satisfaction and rewards him with genuine friendships.

Along his academic and athletic journey, Allan felt lucky to have the support and encouragement of two special teachers. One of them, Melvin Soong, was his fifth-grade teacher at Kailua Elementary School. Allan said that he remembered Mr. Soong's first day as his new teacher. Mr. Soong wore his white short-sleeved dress shirt, a tie and black-rimmed glasses. Before long, Allan knew that he was blessed to have Mr. Soong as his teacher. Despite the fact that Allan was kalohi (rascal) at times, Mr. Soong saw in his student what Allan had not seen for himself – an academic and athletic future. With Mr. Soong's encouragement and belief in him, Allan began to realize that he had something valuable to offer, and learned that communication – letting people know what was in your head and heart was important in getting the support you needed to accomplish your goals. Mr. Soong told Allan, "What I like about you is that you're not afraid to ask questions. Ask and you will receive. The only stupid question is the one not asked." Allan never forgot that.

When Allan went to Kailua High School, he was lucky to have Harry Murai as his math teacher and basketball coach. Mr. Murai encouraged Allan to concentrate on his studies and to sharpen his athletic skills on the basketball court. To inspire Allan, who was then 6'1" ft. tall, Mr. Murai gave him a picture of an all-American football player, Ted Hendricks, who happened to be 6'7"ft. tall. Mr. Murai shared how this all-American player attained his success through hard work in the classroom and on the basketball court. He wanted to see Allan do the same thing. With Mr. Murai's support and guidance, and Allan's determination to succeed, he went on to Chaminade University, where he majored in education and starred on the basketball court. In his fourth year there, Allan -- at 6' 7" ft. tall at the time -- was an acclaimed athlete on the Chaminade University championship basketball team.   And Although Allan couldn't have predicted that he would be as tall as the all-American Mr. Murai talked about, he knew that he had soared far above any goal that he had set for himself. Mr. Murai's work with Allan had certainly come to fruition.

Upon graduation, Allan was besieged with offers to play professional basketball in Europe and the Philippines, but declined the offers to stay home in

Hawaii and become an educator. Allan says he never regretted his decision to do that. His graduation from college was a special event – he was the first in his family to graduate from college – and that gave him great satisfaction. Through his own educational experiences, he realized the tremendous influence an educator could have on students to change their lives for the better. He wanted to do just that.

With a Bachelor's Degree in Psychology and Education, Allan started his work with youth. He became involved in organizations and activities specifically targeted at youth, such as: conducting leadership workshops for kids, taking on the role as YMCA Program Director, working with the DOE State Student Activities Specialist in coordinating activities for students, helping with the Drug Abuse and Resistant Education (DARE) at schools, working with the Adult Friends for Youth Transitional Program, Kalihi Palama Health Center, The Bobby Benson Center, and Alu Like's Youth Program. Eventually Allan received a Master's Degree in Counseling and Guidance. Today, he continues to offer positive messages to students at school assemblies, and is currently an Out-Reach Counselor at Farrington High School, as well as the head coach for the boys' basketball team at the School.

While working with students at risk, Allan arranged a visit to the Oahu Community Correctional Center

(OCCC) to talk with inmates to gain insight as to life within bars. When one of the students asked a big, burly inmate, "What is the one thing you've regretted?" his response was, "that I didn't tell my dad that I loved him." The inmate then challenged all of the students to go home and tell their parents that they loved them. After the OCCC session, Allan gave the students their homework assignment. He told the students to take up the challenge and tell their parents that they loved him. The students balked. They felt themselves too macho to do that. This wasn't something they normally would do – with anybody, much less their parents. Allan insisted. The students agreed only if Allan would also go home and tell his dad the same thing. Allan agreed.

However, he found that to be a challenging task, because as a married man living away from home, he hadn't told his parents that he loved them for a long time --- not after he and his brother grew up and left their home. But Allan was willing to do that and besides, he had given his word to the students. That night he called his parents and told them that he was coming over to visit them. When he got there, they were just finishing their dinner. They were surprised that he was there on a work day, but they were happy to see him. They talked about many things – perhaps Allan was trying to build up enough courage to do what he had promised his students. As Allan got up to leave their home, he told them, "I really came over to tell the two of you that I love you." His father looked at him somewhat surprised at hearing this, and asked, "What do you want, son?" Allan said "Nothing dad, you gave my everything I ever needed. I just wanted to tell you folks how much I loved you." Then his dad replied, "I love you too, son!" His mother watching all of this between Allan and his father, followed him to the door and went out to the garage. As he walked to his car, his mom hugged him tightly and as Allan walked to his car, she cried out, "Son, I love you!" He looked at his precious mother, in her light pink nightgown waving at him and yelled back, "I love you too! Mom". That was the last time he saw his mother alive. Allan was grateful that he had the opportunity to let his parents know how much he loved them.

In 1995 Allan started Positive Connections, a non-profit organization that brings students together to share common goals and interests. Initially, the activities were funded by Aloha Care and Kamaina Kids, and eventually became a program sponsored by the Hawaii State Department of Education. As part of the program, Allan conducted student assemblies, which provided students with inspirational messages and showcased student talent from around the state.

As an experienced educator and father of three grown children, Allan believes in the power that one adult can have on a student's life. So he continues to share his gifts of *aloha* with students here in Hawaii

ALOHA

(love)

`O ke aloha, he manawa ho`opā hou `ia, mohala hou!

A heart retouched, blooms again!

and on the mainland. Allan's goal is to have a
National Youth Summit here in Hawaii – so that students from around the United States can see the
beauty that Hawaii has to offer and feel the spirit of
its people.   It is that spirit that Allan carries wherever
he goes – to help other people see the beauty in the
world and their part in it.

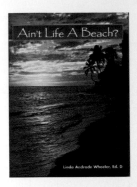

Discover these other
winning titles by
Dr. Wheeler and
share them with
your friends, family
and team.

To order copies,
telephone
Successories of Hawaii
Consumer Sales at:
1-800-471-9808
or in Hawaii, call
808-592-6400.

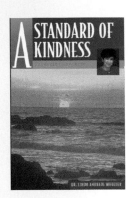

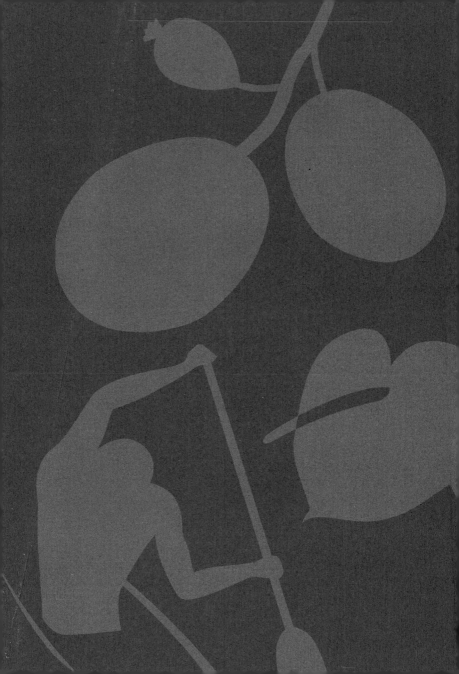